Tuscan Echoes

Tuscan Echoes:

A Season in Italy

Mary Jo —
In deepest appreciation —
Enjoy!

Mark G. Smith

Almar Books
Ocean Isle Beach, NC

Almar Books, Ocean Isle Beach, NC 28469
www.almarbooks.com

First Edition, 2003

09 08 07 06 05 04 03   7 6 5 4 3 2 1

Printed in Canada

The publishers have generously given permission to use a
quotation from the following copyrighted work:

From *The Virgin's Knot* by Holly Payne, copyright © 2002 by
Holly Payne. Used by permission of Dutton, a division of the
Penguin Group (USA) Inc.

Applied for Library of Congress Control Number

ISBN: 0-9740983-0-2

Book and Jacket Design by October Publishing

Cover & interior photos: Mark G. Smith
Author photo: Barbara Parkins

For my mother, Helen Dodge Dehnke Smith, whose
laughter echoes still amongst
the hills of Tuscany

and

in memory of Dr. Gary S. Jacobs

Sometimes there are places in the world we have never been but the minute we step into them we are forever changed. We have native towns, houses where we grew up and return to now and then, but somehow, something overtakes us when we set foot in our homeland. Some call it the karmic debt land and we know it better than the places with which we are most familiar. A crooked tree, a bend in the road, the way a mountain whispers. We need no road sign here because we already know the way, and everything at once becomes home.

—Holly Payne, *The Virgin's Knot*

Contents

I imagine that a Medici will suddenly open wide an ancient window, wavy with age, from one of the high galleries of the Uffizi.

Acknowledgements

For all that Italians give, their passion for living, for a way of life that is beautiful and free, I thank them. The critical editorial and design skills, as well as the encouragement of both Nikki Smith and Nicki Leone at October Publishing made this entire process not only a great learning experience, they made it a joy. My gratitude is extended to the employees of Homebase Abroad, who found a treasure of a place to call home. The people who work at GIDEC in Florence provided the service to my rental apartment. Their support and encouragement were invaluable.

Barbara came to Italy at the beginning of the season. She has never faltered in her belief that our hearts discover their truest expression when they find home. Flowers she planted on the terrace of the apartment lived through that long season; the petals of those flowers will grace the visions of many visitors yet to come. For her inspiration and faith, I extend my deepest affection and appreciation.

Heartfelt thanks go to: Hugo at the Café Arno on Via de' Bardi; Paolo Azzarri and his family at the Delicatesse Azzarri on Borgo San Jacopo; Ivano at La Bottega del Gelato on Via Por Santa Maria; Fabio, and the entire Baudone family, at Trattoria Bibe on Via delle Bagnese; Luisa Fabiani and her family, owners of my favorite shop on Via de' Bardi; Giancarlo Mordini, Norbert Weinheimer, and Joaquim Temme. Each of you welcomed in a stranger whose life was forever enriched by your kindness, generosity, and support.

Alma Tcruz and I stood on a balcony of the Hotel Excelsior many years ago. She told me that this book had to be written. For her faith and vision, I extend my sincere thanks. Catherine Pyke and Elaine Jaynes have read through too many drafts of this work to number. For their observations and unending support, I thank them. I also wish to thank Bea Kerloff and Edith Isaac Rose, founders of Art Workshop International. Were it not for their tireless work, those two weeks in Assisi could not have happened. Michael Cunningham provided inspiration for a lifetime in Assisi. I cannot thank him enough.

I owe immeasurable thanks to the people of Malmantile, especially the Guarnieri family and Signora Bianca. They know of the villa on the hill, and it is to that place my memory returns more often than any other.

I wish to thank my parents, Dane Marshall Smith and Helen Dehnke Smith and my brother, Brian Marshall Smith. Many years ago they brought me to Tuscany. It was the beginning of a never ending love affair with Italy.

Finally, to Alan: my gratitude knows no bounds.

Prologo

ITALY. MANY YEARS AGO, THIS COUNTRY OF MELODIOUS language, stunning natural beauty, and friendly, open people conquered my heart and shaped a dream.

In the late 1950s our family lived along the Tyrrhenian Sea, not far from Florence. It was during those early years that I came to know the Italian people—and their country—in a deeply personal way.

We often accepted gracious invitations for dinner from our landlord and his family. Their living room had large western-facing windows that welcomed in late afternoon light. The air was filled with the smells of the fire and of the kitchen's roasting meats. After dinner, the landlord's wife, Anna, would sit at a baby grand piano near the windows and play music of the Italian masters while we sat satiated and dumbstruck by the beauty around us.

These were times when we were wrapped in the intimacy of Italian life, times when the country seeped into our souls. A love of Italy pulsed through our hearts, forming the core of memories with which it continues to bless us.

Thirty years of visits to this richly diverse land have further reinforced my passion for all things Italian. I've walked the corridors and countryside of Italian history, spent hours in museums full of too many masterpieces to recall, and enjoyed espressos in cafés near unnamed piazzas. I have spent time talking with shopkeepers about the weather, the city, and the river, of politics, music, and love. When I have driven the roads of Italy, umbrella pines along the roads flashed by; the towers of Renaissance churches spiked the sky; ancient Roman villas or centuries-old aqueducts faded behind me. The beautiful soul of Italy seeped into me so deeply that I had to return to live, as a *semi-Fiorentino*, (nearly Florentine). Every year the desire to return, to live there, grew stronger and stronger. Two years ago, my opportunity arrived.

With the help of a small U.S. based company, Homebase Abroad, I made arrangements to lease an apartment in the center of Florence, steps from its ancient bridge, the Ponte Vecchio. The small retreat, directly on the River Arno, offered views over the city in every direction, a large terrace, and privacy. And so, on the first day of May, bags packed and plans set, I set off to bask for months in the spiritual and soulful power of Italy.

Florence was my home for that season. There was a two-week trip into the heart of Umbria, and a few precious days were set aside to visit another glorious Italian city, Venice. I spent the latter part of the season exploring the region of Tuscany. A few friends visited. All in all, I lived a life once only dreamed of. I wrote this book, and I flourished in the moments that so many take for granted.

Time became the gift that provided opportunities to take in quiet moments and places, to capture the special essence of Italian life. Even now, I need only close my eyes to feel the heat of that Tuscan season. There were days when an infinite clear blue sky soared overhead, hot breezes shrilled the cypresses of cloisters, olive trees shaded fields of straw punctuated by bright red poppies, and aisles of Chianti grapes marched forever up every hill. On every day, in every corner turned, a new discovery was made; with every museum entered or church visited, there were thousands of other events that reached out to be remembered. As the seasons turned, leaves blew at my feet and, eventually, the rains of fall arrived.

My hope was for this beautiful land and her people to teach me, to show me new sights, new sounds, to renew a tired soul. The Italians, as they always have done, welcomed me in.

This book is my gift to Italy and to those of you who love her. It is my hope that a poetic soul will be discovered, and that you will find within these pages some deeper understanding of what makes this place rest so powerfully, yet so softly, upon our hearts. To those who have yet to visit Italy, Tuscany in particular, it is my hope that you will be inspired to a moment when you simply say, "I must go."

Firenze

Rising

A NEW DAY BEGINS IN FLORENCE, AND THE GARDENS OF the Boboli beckon as they always do on my first day in the city. There are few people out after this morning's bristling May shower. The political and artistic heart of the city, the Piazza della Signoria, is but a short walk from the most famous bridge in the world, the Ponte Vecchio. The offices in the ancient Palazzo della Signoria (palace of the governing body) face a square that contains masterworks of art, cafés, and many of the city's most successful and well-known businesses.

Outside the Café Rivori, jacketed waiters sweep remnants of rain from a wooden deck and iron-black stone patio in preparation for another busy day. Across the square a young man pushes a four-wheeled cart full of who-knows-what up into the center of the Piazza and begins to open his stand for the day's business. High up in the façade of the Palazzo a window opens. A well-dressed man leans out to face the brisk fresh air of morning with a stretch and a long look across the open space at his feet. For innumerable mornings Florentines, Tuscans, Italians have started their days like this. As I stroll in front of the fountain of *Neptune* on this late spring morning I think of the millions who have visited here, recall the many writers and artists whose feet have walked upon this lively stage.

The way to the Boboli Gardens takes me across the Ponte Vecchio, and along the shop-lined Via Guicciardini to the artists' stalls that line the grand piazza in front of the Pitti Palace. Further on, as I approach the obelisk in the Piazza di San Felice, I imagine Elizabeth Barrett Browning penning "Casa Guidi Windows" from the small villa across the square. I visualize her pen scrolling across the paper as she wrote:

> I heard last night a little child go singing
> 'Neath Casa Guidi windows, by the church,
> "O bella liberta, O bella!"

Just down the street is a small back entrance to the Boboli Gardens, a simple iron gate; 4000 lira and I'm in.

These gardens were laid out after the Medici family purchased the land in 1549. When Lorenzo the Magnificent's grandson, Lorenzo Duke of Urbino, married Catherine of France, she took it upon herself to oversee the creation of the Palazzo Pitti's formal gardens. The appearance of the gardens as they stand today is a direct result of her work. In 1737, the last blood relation of the Medici Dynasty, Gian Gastone, died. His wife, Anna Maria Luisa (of Saxe-Lauenburg), inherited all of the remaining Medici palazzos and villas. It was her generous donation (known as the "Treaty", or "Convention of the Family") that gave the entire artistic heritage of the Medici Dynasty to Florence, thus assuring the city's vast artistic treasure. Included in this decree were the Palazzo Pitti and the Boboli Gardens.

Opened to the people of Florence in 1766, it was Catherine's passionate vision that formed the beginnings of *Il Boboli*. Florence's green beauty, her verdant soul, continues to thrive here. Every time I enter, I see something new.

Many statues inside the garden are draped in white-netted fabric that is placed over a wooden frame. The structure surrounds and protects statues while they are being restored. Workers hide within, their voices muted and happy. When the pieces are, at long last, revealed, they appear new, even with missing fragments. They breathe new life into the garden.

The spectacular Viottolone, known as "Cypress Alley," was planted in the early 1600s. The trees along this magnificent wide-graveled alleyway are now nearly sixty feet high. They have grown in relative calm through wars and republics, and continue to grow, undisturbed, flourishing. As I walk, I imagine voices of the Court of the Republic whispering between the boxwood hedges, dancing between the cypresses.

At the far end of the Viottolone is the *Oceanus Fountain*, a place where waters dance now, sadly, only on the weekends. Today there are a few families enjoying a picnic. Lovers whisper close by. Near the fountain are *The Grotesques*, three statues in a small side garden that represent Pride, Avarice, and Lust. Their complex postures invite closer inspection. Their exaggerated faces remind me of the work of Leonardo da Vinci, a man whose sketches reflect an unerring eye for the comedy and tragedy in everyone's lives.

This is the southwestern limit of the garden. A huge iron gate, built into what were once walls that protected fifteenth-century Florence, opens out to the Piazza della Porta Romana. The cacophony of traffic noise that I encounter is out of place in this quiet space. I turn away from the gate and stroll up the path that leads to the summit of the garden.

The Boboli, while my favorite, is but one of numerous city gardens. The Villas Torrigiani, Corsini, Leonardo, and others, all provide gardens of rest and beauty. They invite you to take a break in the shade of a rose-trellised arbor, to stroll through thickets of lush green where pathways are dotted with roundels of light.

It is growing late. The long rays of the setting sun cut across the garden paths. I realize that this first day is coming, all too quickly, to a close. I make my way to the gate with a promise to myself to return as soon as I can.

By the time I reach the maze of streets at the south end of the Ponte Vecchio, I can feel the fatigue of jet lag and the numbing excitement begin to fade. I retreat to my apartment to prepare dinner and think, again, of the Boboli. It is a garden I encourage everyone to visit often. Her tenderly-attended plantings and fountains, and the Palazzo she protects, are not only mute testaments to this city of art, life, and love, they are also a wonderful place in which to discover the verdant heart of Florence.

Fresh chicken breasts, cloves of garlic, olive oil, spinach, and ruby red tomatoes fill the small refrigerator of my apartment. I took care of my daily shopping in the neighborhood this morning, and I look forward to a simple, fresh meal of the finest that local businesses offer. Signora Luisa Fabiani and her family run the vegetable stand on the street that parallels the river near my apartment. They have owned and operated the same fruit and vegetable stand for generations. Her bright, lively face and carefree laugh fill my eyes and ears with great joy. She is the product of a life lived with passion for her family, their business, and for the city of Florence. I look forward to spending more time with her as the season progresses.

After a superb meal, I clean up the tiny kitchen and head upstairs. My bedroom windows offer unobstructed views of the city. I can see across to the south face of the Uffizi Gallery. It's nearing 9 P.M., and as I lean out of the window to take in the fresh air, music rises to my ears. In the midst of the open piazza at the Uffizi Gallery, the center of Italian art, there is a young man playing an electric violin to pre-recorded background music.

Some of the pieces he plays are recognizable: the theme from *Cinema Paradiso*, a Bach piece. There are many others. The music draws people into the small piazza.

Lovers sit, arm in arm, moving deeply into the soul of the city, learning one with the other. They appear transfixed by the dark, the place, the music, and the moment. I imagine that a Medici will suddenly open wide an ancient window, wavy with age, from one of the high galleries in the Uffizi. I close my eyes and picture the crowds that have, over the ages, gathered in this same piazza to celebrate the marriage of a famous son or daughter. At this moment, we are all united to this city of inexorable beauty. I listen for a few more moments and close my eyes as the music wraps itself around the dark cool air of evening.

Finally, fatigue overtakes me. Notes from across the river drift through the open window. A gentle breeze whispers through the curtains of the room, and I find rest with dreams of gardens, music, and art accompanying me in sleep; Eighteen weeks, in a city of dreams, lie ahead.

The Piazza del Duomo

ONE OF THE GREATEST JOYS OF A MORNING OUT IN Florence is taking time to sit in a café, drink a cappuccino, and have a fresh pastry. The cafés typically have hedges around them, high enough to afford privacy, yet also offering a view. One of the grandest of the city's many piazzas is the one surrounding the Duomo (cathedral).

The Duomo of Florence (also called the Cathedral of Santa Maria del Fiore), the Baptistry, and Campanile (bell tower) rise up suddenly from the Piazza del Duomo. I often walk out from one of the ancient streets surrounding the glorious Piazza to find myself only a few feet from the base of these stunning, huge, buildings. Their splendor and scale never cease to amaze me.

It is a beautiful clear morning, and a table at Café da Scudieri is an inviting place for a light breakfast. As crowds and individuals pass by, I am reminded of how much people walk here. They stroll piazzas, walk the streets, shop, conduct the affairs of business, and find their way to and from their homes. People push bicycles across the stone pavement. The ever-present Polizia saunter past. People push strollers, gently leading their passengers to the best views.

Walkers in gym shoes slip by gingerly seeking the sights. There are tourists in leather sandals awed by the suddenness of such architectural majesty.

The City of Florence provides locations for tourist assistance. Two women in immaculate blue uniforms staff the location in the Piazza del Duomo. They smile and help tourists as they come and go.

"Where is the Baptistery?" one asks.

"It's right there, in front of you," they reply.

"Which way to Piazza San Marco?" They point the way.

Most of the uniformed officers speak several languages. I overhear them speaking in English, Italian, French, and German. Tourism draws large numbers of visitors to these places of historical significance and, since motorized traffic is now prohibited in this Piazza, people move easily across the large open space.

Walking is a time-honored tradition in Italy. Most every evening, the citizens of villages and towns gather to stroll together, to share the day, to quietly join in conversation. A gentleman passes by with a dustpan and broom. Neatly dressed in blue cotton shirt, gray slacks, and shined black shoes he patiently cleans the stones of the Piazza. Two older women stroll by, arm in arm, hair perfectly set, both in fine knitted suits. They are deeply engaged in conversation, their smiles signaling some secretive news shared within the confines of their friendship. A Japanese group passes by, silently honoring the beauty of this place. Tourists from the United States walk past the café, one group dutifully following a tour guide who holds aloft a plastic sunflower. They are silent. Heads raised, eyes alight, they take in the sights around them, anticipating the beauty of what lies ahead—the Duomo, the Baptistery. Who knows?

And so it goes, this movement of peoples in the Piazza. Across cultures, oceans, and ages, each seeks their own memory in this city filled with visions, in this city of art. For centuries it has been so. Visitors have been drawn to the majesty and the splendor that Florence offers up in such vast array. To take it all in, one needs a lifetime, not days. Even so, what each remembers this day will be shared across families, countries, and continents, enticing the uninitiated.

I pay my bill, leave the table, and walk towards the entrance to the Duomo. The line has dwindled from the usual wait of several minutes to mere seconds, and I enter. Beams of light pierce deeply into the farthest corners of the interior, illuminating chapels and altars of profound religious expression.

The cathedrals of Italy, Florence particularly, are cavernous structures. At one time, the massive pediments of the Duomo supported numerous shrines to as many saints as the edifice could hold. Santa Croce, another of the city's many churches was so divided, as was Santa Maria Novella and many others. The effect on the architectural simplicity of the design, its essential, spiritual intent, was confused and jumbled. Worship at the time was worship for the sake of political and familial alliance rather than the spiritual well being of the believers. The interior layout of cathedrals was of little concern.

In the late fifteenth century most of Italy's churches were reconfigured. Aisles once crowded with a multitude of altars were cleared of clutter. In the Duomo of Florence, five apses were completed, each with five chapels. The financing for these magnificent rooms came from the wealthiest families of the city. The interiors of churches were made into grand and glorious light-filled spaces. In the duomo's of Pisa, Florence, Siena, or in the simple clarity of churches like San Mineato, San Francesco, or Ognissanti, the act of worship was once again enhanced by a profusion of light.

This morning in the Duomo I hear the shuffle of sandals and shoes on the ancient floor: a priest walks by engaged in a quiet conversation with a parishioner; a small group of tourists stands, agape, at the immensity of the dome; different languages, whispered, echo softly up into the vastness of this celebrated cathedral. Even today, the Duomo gathers together the faithful and the curious.

Italy's religious places have been rocked by wars, plague, and vague comings and goings of political and religious fervor. Yet they still stand. As I walk slowly to the doors of the Duomo, the message that I feel the building breathe into me is: *Whatever your belief, I stand as testimony to the faith that for centuries has enlightened believers' souls and has kept the spirit of this city alive.*

Florentine Ghosts

IT IS THE LAST WEEKEND IN MAY. MANY PRIVATE
Florentine homes and gardens have been opened for a rare
public glimpse into their usually secluded interiors. The
Giardino Torrigiani, the Palazzos Ricasoli, Guicciardini,
Frescobaldi, and many others across the city, are open to the
delight of surprised visitors who come upon ancient oak
gates in the street. Guests are often stunned to silence by
the ineffable beauty hidden behind such imposing façades.

The Palazzo Corsini, built in the fifteenth century, is
located near the Ponte alle Carraia, one of the many bridges
that cross the Arno downriver from the Ponte Vecchio. This
Sunday afternoon the Palazzo is open to visitors. I step
through the arched courtyard gateway and cross the
graveled garden. As I enter the palace, several young
Florentines dressed in fifteenth-century costumes float across
the hallway before me. A man dressed in a yellow silk jacket
glides past mullioned windows, across the black and white
marble floor, and joins a group of dancers. A couple, dressed
in centuries-old silks and wigs, sits silently, staring out doors
opened to an afternoon breeze. Lights from behind cast a

luminous glow around them and they become a timeless portrait. It seems the ghosts of Florence have come alive.

A quartet plays period music on what appear to be original instruments, adding to the warp in time, of not being sure what year or place we are in. Dancers shimmer amidst the music and soft haze of light. Their faces betray thoughts of balls and masquerades from centuries ago, when such palaces hosted gatherings of power and prestige.

I stand for a few minutes to take this all in, and then turn to go. Stones crunch under my feet as I cross the graveled courtyard. I turn around and wait at the gate. I feel, at times like these, that ghosts *can* be real. They move over pavement centuries old; their feet float above the stones, unheard, at all hours of the day and night.

Today at the Palazzo Corsini I have been given the rare gift of seeing those ghosts live. Their spirits inhabit the hearts of the young costumed dancers inside the Palazzo. Yet another generation shows their appreciation for the history and beauty of this city. As they dance into the waning light of this superb spring evening, I depart, smiling in appreciation for another unforgettable gift of Florence.

Gates of Paradise

A POSTER ON AN ANCIENT WALL ATTRACTS MY ATTENTION. "The music of the Medici Court" is to be performed at a church on the Via Por Santa Maria. A tiny street is tucked into a quiet corner off the main route from the Ponte Vecchio to the Piazza della Signoria. The Church of Santo Stefano al Ponte, consecrated in 1233, is now the home of the Orchestra da Camera Fiorentina. This evening's concert is being given by a quartet playing on period, Renaissance instruments, accompanied by a soprano soloist.

At 7:45 in the evening I take my place in the last row of seats and study the interior of the church. It is full of restored rococo-fluted columns with cherubic upper corners. Family chapels line each side of the sanctuary. A stairway with intricately carved balustrades leads up to the high altar. Five musicians enter and take their places. They are dressed in period costumes based upon those worn in the courts of Cosimo and Lorenzo di Medici. There are rich velvet brocades, sweeping turban-like head wraps, and white linen blouses. The program guides us through the music of the early Medici courts and includes a choral composition written by Cosimo. There is a moment in the program where the soprano leaves the high altar and, book in hand, reads from Dante's *Divine Comedy* in the original Italian.

As she descends the stairs the church goes silent, save for the rustle of her long skirt on the marble floor and the soft shuffle of her shoes on the stone. Dante's words rise from her clear, melodic voice. I listen and imagine the long dead, momentarily freed by this ancient language, once again dancing among the candle-cast shadows. Dante's words fill the space, each intimation understood even in this, a foreign tongue. The performer glides across the floor, and the last words spoken, ". . . We read no more that day," echo and fade. She takes her place at the top of the stairs, surrounded by silenced players. There is no applause. Rather, a quiet reverence settles around us. The remainder of the performance is filled with breathtaking music. At the close of the concert, the audience departs through a door centered in the back of the church, and the performers retreat behind the glorious main altar. I choose to remain alone in the midst of this quiet place.

Candles flicker atop candelabra. Frescoes dim in the waning light. As I rise and turn to go, a shaft of moonlight enters from high above the church entrance. It casts its pale blue beam onto the floor. I am overcome by the simple beauty of the moment. Outside the church, the noise and clamor of people on their way to and from the Ponte Vecchio breaks the spell. The magic created this evening must now find residence somewhere in a newly-lighted corner of my memory.

San Mineato al Monte

THE CHURCH OF SAN MINEATO AL MONTE STANDS HIGH above Florence on the Monte alle Croce (Mount of the Cross). You can see the church's white and green façade from almost any point in the city. It was atop this hill, in the year A.D. 1018, that monks seeking refuge and privacy built their first place of worship.

On this beautiful afternoon in June, I find myself in need of retreat from the city. The number thirteen bus drops me at Piazzale Michelangelo, a place where the high view out over the city is tinged with the haze of summer's heat. I begin making my way towards the church. There are vendors and carts in great abundance along the street.

I wonder what this place was like when that first church was built. How did they build it? Where did the wood and stone, the carvers, the makers of mosaic and of bells all come from, and where did they go when the work was completed?

There are well-worn, steep steps up to the entrance of the church. The façade above me, as I climb, is a glory of white and green marble. Centered above the main doors is a mosaic of glass and gold with the figures of Christ and Mary, and on the opposite side, St. Minias. I have seen this mosaic reflect back the long reach of the setting sun, the rays of light sparkling brightly, suffusing the haze over the city with glints of gold and tiny bursts of light. Up close it is even more breathtaking. I notice a sign for the cemetery and decide to walk through it before exploring the interior of the church.

The Cimitero Monumentale (Monumental Cemetery) has existed since the first church was built on this site. It is here that many families of Tuscany and Florence have built intricate memorials to their loved ones. The cemetery is huge and now occupies the grounds south, east, and north behind the church. The moving tributes to those buried here are too numerous to count.

One memorial depicts the body of Christ on a double crucifix, his oversized form all but indiscernible by the grotesque deformity of his passion and death. Another monument is a life-sized sculpture of a young couple. Someone has placed a fresh gardenia in the woman's outstretched hand. Her partner, a handsome uniformed young man, holds a live rose in a hand that clasps hers. I wonder who it is that places these fresh flowers? The couples' smiles are a reminder of whom they were when they met. He died in 1944, she in 1945, both victims among the millions who perished during the war. In another memorial, a naked young man lies prostrate in grief, his hands holding flowers he can never give, his face melded into the stone. There is a monument to a sculptor, his epitaph simply his name and *Scultore Tuscano* (Tuscan sculptor). A bronze Christ rises from a shattered tomb, his left leg raised as he prepares to stand again, resurrected, his pierced side and hands visible. As I walk towards the gate of the cemetery I notice a small group gathered for a funeral. It reminds me that life and death do indeed go on in this city known for crowds of tourists, pageants, and food.

The silence here seems interrupted only by the song of birds, the crunch of the occasional sandaled passerby, the ringing of church bells, and the occasional sliding of marble over another resting soul. I return to the front of the church and enter the sanctuary.

The floor is tiled with grave markers, each outlined in deep green marble. There are over a hundred of them, some well worn. Others, along the wall, seem almost new. I always walk the green lines between them. Something in my past reveres the graves, and I can't walk on them. At 5:30 the bells begin to toll; their deep and thunderous voices vibrate the floors and arches of the church.

I continue to study the fifteenth-century mosaic in the dome high above the main altar. There are cypress trees, the Lion of Florence, the figure of Christ, and the haloed faces of his disciples. The bell's last notes fade inside the church.

There is a shuffle of sandals on stone coming from down in the crypt. Three chanted notes rise from the candlelit interior. Unexpectedly they appear, monks in stark white-hooded robes. One carries a cross; the others follow two by two until all sixteen are in their places. They stand quietly. A single voice chants a phrase, and the church is filled with the music of Gregorian chant. The sound fills the space, rises up to the high wooden ceiling, and caresses the brilliant mosaic dome. The mass continues, sung chant-on-chant, and the worshipers find respite in the liturgy and music.

Such surprises as these make Florence a place of majesty and mystery for me. In churches throughout the city, on this summer's eve, mass is being celebrated. I feel immeasurably lucky to be in this ancient place, wrapped by the sounds of medieval chants. For an hour that passes as a minute, I sit in a meditation of image and music. By the end of the service, the long reach of the afternoon sun streams through the doors of the church. The service draws quietly to a close. The monks rise and form into pairs, side by side, as the chants continue. They disappear into a hallway off of the crypt. What remains behind is the sound of their sandals, shuffling on stone, and the last whispered notes of their song. I remain in the church for a few more minutes before deciding to depart.

Amazing.

I walk down the front stairs, along the street, towards the Piazzale Michelangelo.

The Café Michelangelo perches above Florence, just up the hill from the Piazzale. As I study the menu I am suddenly overwhelmed by the view. It is breathtaking. Along the edge of the hill are segments of walls that once surrounded Florence. An ancient stone wall angles up a nearly forty-five-degree hill towards Fort Belvedere. From there it angles away from the city, following the base ramparts of the Fort. At the end of the ramparts it rejoins the wall above the Boboli Gardens.

A Renaissance palazzo is silhouetted against the orange western sky; verdant green trees stand in its garden. Closer to me a stone loggia, covered with a plethora of blossoms, encloses a garden. One lone umbrella pine stands sentinel on the far edge. A graveled path lined with lemon trees leads away from the precipice, and at its far end are six magnificent Italian cypresses. A small guesthouse, opposite the main villa, perfectly balances the view.

A patchwork of villas, in various earth colors, fills the valley below. One is the color of deep ochre. A large blue awning protects its entranceway. A small garden, hedged by tall oleanders in bloom guards its south-facing wall. A pink villa with three terraces pokes out from below the Fort and, closer in, is a dark orange villa with forest green shutters. Planters are filled to overflowing with germaniums of every conceivable hue. In the low center of the valley is a large olive grove. Polished emerald green leaves contrast against the dry yellow of cut hay.

A pizza smothered in fresh porcini mushrooms, succulent sliced tomatoes, slivers of Parma ham, and fresh grated Parmesan cheese arrives at my table. A glass of Chianti and a bottle of mineral water complete the meal. A farmer on his tractor appears in the olive grove and, as I continue to slowly enjoy a marvelous meal, he begins to tend to his fields. The sun begins to fade and, as I settle the bill and head back to the apartment, a few last rays of light strike the windows of the Uffizi gallery. It is a sign. Tomorrow I will finally visit the home of Italian art.

The easy walk down the Via del Monte alle Croci (Way of the Mount of the Cross) is filled with memories of a resting place, the music of the ages, and the colors of the Tuscan rainbow.

Gallery 10, Uffizi

THE UFFIZI. THE LONG UPPER CORRIDORS IN THIS famous building used to be the *uffizi* (offices), of the Medici family. The great wealth that they acquired is evident in the scale of the building. It connects the Arno with the Piazza della Signoria and its center courtyard of high arches and covered loggia is now decorated with sculptures of Florence's most famous sons.

The ancient offices have been transformed, over time, to house one of the richest collections of art and sculpture in the world. It is the crown jewel of Italy's artistic heritage. Room twenty-five holds Michelangelo's *The Holy Family*. Room two has Giotto's masterpiece, *The Ognissanti Madonna*. Room after room is full of the greatest Italian and western European art.

Room Ten, one of four rooms primarily housing the work of Sandro Botticelli, is known for what has become his most famous painting, *Primavera* (Spring). Most visitors long to see *Primavera*; I have fallen for another Botticelli altogether. Near the huge canvas of *Primavera* is the work that captivates me: it is Botticelli's *Annunciation*. A masterpiece of light, posture, and movement, the painting captures the moment when the angel appears in Mary's chambers. The angel kneels before her, and Mary leans towards the angel, one arm and hand outstretched. The angel's wings are of ephemeral sheerness. He looks up at her with a gaze of deference and warmth, of kindness and patience. A delicate, sheer drape crosses his neck and shoulder, one end lying carelessly on the floor of the room, the other layered against his shoulders, shimmering off the canvas.

Mary's gaze is directed down to the floor and reflects a certain shyness and trepidation. Her posture, which curves to the right, is balanced by the extension of her arm. She reaches out, as if to indicate her hesitation to believe the angel's message. Her fingers rise above the level of her hand, each finger a subtle sign of shock, temerity, and disbelief. Mary stands above the angel, her head tilted to the side, her draped garments flowing in the breeze of an April day in the hills above Galilee.

It is a powerful work.

Botticelli's *Annunciation* is but one of the hidden treasures of the Uffizi. Many others remain to be discovered amidst the maze of streets that connect the life of the city. As I leave the Uffizi, after hours of rewarding exploration, I turn towards the Piazza della Signoria. In the Loggia dei Lanzi (named after the Lancers in the service of Cosimo de Medici I) is one particular statue that has drawn me back numerous times over the past several weeks.

Perseus

BENVENUTO CELLINI BEGAN HIS LONG STUDIES AND artistic career in the workshops of jewelers. It was with those special artisans that he learned the fine attention to detail and the finesse of form that so characterizes his work. Under the protective cover of the Loggia dei Lanzi, which lies between the Uffizi Gallery and the Piazza de la Signoria, stands what many consider to be his masterpiece, *Perseus*.

I have spent hours studying this masterwork. The complexity of it is amazing; Perseus stands, eyes downward, holding the severed, snake-wrapped head of Medusa in his left hand. Across his torso stretches a strap upon which Cellini signed his name. Perseus' face is confident, serene, and sure. His raised arm flows into his shoulders: muscles tensed under taut skin, the nape of the neck covered by rivulets cut into sensuously curled hair. The back, curved and almost cocky in its posture, sleekly slips towards the buttocks. The right arm holds a deeply curved sword, its sharp edge still dripping blood. The hand holding the sword appears almost at ease, not tense or tight.

The remains of Medusa curve about the base of Perseus' right foot; his left foot rests on her chest. Medusa's right arm reaches back behind the body, as if to hold the remains in place. Even in death she lassoes and holds the figure of Perseus, a circular epitaph to the final struggle and the end of her life.

As I sit staring at the statue, one of the uniformed guards walks up and asks me if I am an artist. I tell her that, as a writer, I hope to capture in words the beauty of this particular sculpture. She smiles and shares with me that many women love *Perseus*.

I ask why.

She shakes her hand across the front of her body, something that I have always identified as particularly Italian, and says, "That butt! How could any woman resist that butt?" I laugh right along with her. She wishes me luck as I direct my gaze back at the base of the piece.

The head of a ram tops each of the base's four corners. Farther down each edge is a goddess in a flowing gown. There follows a curved roundel. Below that, surprisingly, is a pair of finely carved feet and, finally, the base. Each face, each garment, each ram's head is different in composure, design, and stance. Each niche in the base contains a bronze figure and plaque. The statues represent the child Perseus with his mother, Danaë, his father, Jupiter, as well as Minerva and Mercury. The plaques depict various important moments in his life.

The piazza that fronts the Signoria is a mass of people, especially during the afternoon. Visitors crowd the shaded alcoves under the loggia to rest, take pictures, or simply watch the passing throng. Perseus looms above them, holding symbols of loss and gain, all but ignored by the river of humanity that passes below. In the moments of silence, when the piazza stands dark and empty, I believe Perseus lowers the head of Medusa to his side. He rests for only a moment before once again raising high the severed head, hoping that someone will come—not to visit, but to see.

I leave the loggia and wave at the guard who spoke with me earlier. As I stroll into the piazza I notice a couple standing near a café. I approach closely enough to overhear their conversation.

It starts with a glance.

"Oh, this place looks okay."

The restaurants and cafés in Florence display their menus so that potential customers can review it before deciding on a meal. In the Piazza de la Signoria the menus are posted at the piazza entrance to each café.

The woman props her sunglasses up on her head; her husband pulls his down to the end of his nose. Their heads go back. Their eyes squint. His right hand and her left find their way to a hip. One leg thrust out, the reading begins.

"What do they have?"

"Oh, ravioli, spaghetti . . ." the voice trails off.

"Do they have pizza? I wanna pizza."

"Yes, they have pizza."

"Well, maybe we should try this place. Is it expensive?"

"Heck, I don't know. What's 9000 lira worth?"

"Um, let me think. The exchange rate yesterday was 2250 lira to the dollar, so that's, um, about $3.75 I think."

"Doesn't sound bad to me."

Almost in unison their weight shifts from one leg to the other. Sometimes the hands move too, seeking another defensive hip on which to rest.

"Uh, I don't know. There are so many places to eat here. Do you suppose they're more expensive over there, on that side street?"

"I'm not eating on a side street. They're too *dark*, and we might get lost."

"Look, I'm hungry. It says here I can get a pizza for $3.75 and I'm eating. You gonna come in with me?"

"Um, well, alright"

They approach a table in the café. They ask the waiter if they may eat, trying their very best to ask in the local tongue.

"Yes, of course sir and madam, you may sit where you please. Will this table suffice?" he replies in perfect English, effortlessly pointing to a small table near a geranium-filled planter.

Flawless, he doesn't miss a beat.

The experience of eating in a Florentine café can never be underestimated. Years from now this couples' dinner, served with views out over one of the most glorious public spaces in Europe, will still be a treasured moment. Regardless of how visitors approach such meals, they are always greeted with charm, grace, and the best bit of Italian flair. Would that I could join them this evening, but my apartment and a meal of fresh fish and salad await.

Side Streets

SMALL SIDE STREETS CONTAIN THE HEART AND SOUL OF Florentine history. They are lined with entrances to villas and churches, *trattorias* (restaurants), grocery stands, the paraphernalia of daily life. All of them hold surprises.

It is a quiet, late afternoon in June. The direct heat of the sun has passed. Shadows cool the narrow canyons between buildings. I walk down the Via de' Bardi, a small lane directly behind my apartment building, and quietly explore.

The Via de' Bardi starts at a small piazza containing a notable modern statue of St. John the Baptist, the patron saint of Florence. I remember that the city is preparing to celebrate his birthday a few days from now. After the noise of the piazza behind me begins to fade I come to a famous bookbindery and paper maker, El Torchio. A kaleidoscope of richly colored Florentine papers, beautiful note and gift cards, and deep brown leather-bound volumes fill the windows. The owners of El Torchio obtained this shop over thirty years ago, a few brief months after the devastating floods of November 1966. A short distance beyond El

Torchio—and just past the Piazza de' Mozzi—the street becomes Via di San Niccolo.

Classical music floats out from the open door of a jeweler's workshop. Glass cases within display rings of incredible beauty and form. Ancient wooden beams cross the ceiling, and huge wooden columns stand throughout the shop. Allesandro, the owner and designer, sits behind his workbench laboring on another piece of magic. His long black hair skirts the outline of his face; his brow is furrowed in concentration. A deep blue flame hisses an arrow of heat into his work. The heart of a true craftsman resides here, and it shows in the variety and quality of the jewelry. The rings are in fantastic shapes, each named for a famous Italian castle, church, or cloister: "Castello," "Santa Croce," "San Galgano," are but a few that are on display. The music weaves around me. I study each piece in detail. He must appreciate the time I take, for as he looks up, a slight smile rests on his face. I turn to leave, and reenter the world.

Farther along the street is a small altar to the Madonna. A candle flickers against aging frescoes. Fresh cut flowers bloom below the candle. The street levels out and I approach the church of San Niccolò Oltra'Arno. The church is a little known gem. When the troops of Charles V entered Florence, Michelangelo briefly sought refuge in its bell tower. The interior contains the *Trinity* by Neri de Bicci. Candles light the shadowed interior, and recorded Georgian chant floats through the cavernous space. The dark, cool interior offers an inviting retreat. I take time to sit on a pew and enjoy the tranquil peace.

As I retrace my steps up the Via San Niccolò and the Via de' Bardi, I wonder what further stories remain to be discovered along this, and many other byways. The maze of streets within the historic heart of Florence traces the day-to-day commerce and family life of the city, and I look forward to those discoveries.

A small group of people has gathered around the statue of St. John the Baptist near my apartment building. They are decorating it in preparation for the feast of the patron saint of Florence, a day of great celebration and remembrance.

St. John's Birthday

JUNE 24 IS A HIGH HOLY DAY. TODAY, FLORENCE celebrates the feast of its patron saint. Church bells ring every fifteen minutes. It is a cacophonous Sunday. Today, of all days, it is easy to understand how bells used to toll the life of the city.

This afternoon there is a parade, and I walk across the Ponte Vecchio to the Piazza de la Signoria to watch the festivities. The flag tossing is spectacular. Medieval-costumed men toss heraldic flags to each other using the most incredible and convoluted moves. It is ballet. The audience's appreciation is loud, vigorous, and cheerful.

There is a rowing competition on the river Arno, pitting city team against city team, Florence vs. Pisa, San Mineato Sul Arno vs. Montelupo, and others. A well-behaved crowd has gathered to watch. The boats are gorgeous, a deep mahogany color, with seats for ten men. Each man uses a single-bladed paddle. The competition is fierce. City pride is at stake. This is passionate business.

After an hour or so of races, it is announced that the final match, Florence against Pisa, will be settled this evening at 9 P.M., just before the fireworks display. I bow to the heat and retreat to the cool heights of the apartment.

At 8:45 I head down to the river to watch the final boat race. Across the river from the Ponte Vecchio, all the way beyond the Ponte alle Grazie, a distance of at least one-half mile, there is one solid mass of people. Cars are having trouble working their way past the Uffizi Gallery. On my side of the Arno it's not quite as crowded and I find a place to watch. The boats row upriver, nearly even with where I stand. Each craft is lined with tiny lights that make them look like double-stranded diamond bracelets floating in the midnight blue of the river.

The start is clean and, for the majority of the race, the competition is close. The crowds cheer. Water froths along each vessel and a wake becomes their only trace into the darkening distance. There is a gunshot, marking the end of the race. An enormous cheer rises from the crowd: Florence has won.

There are two hot air balloons being inflated upriver past the Ponte alle Grazie, and the firing flames burn rings of orange and red and blue. They look like large, multi-colored light bulbs flickering along and reflecting in the Arno. I again retreat to the terrace of my apartment to watch the fireworks. They are spectacular.

There are bright balls the colors of the Italian flag, red, green, and white. Huge circles of deep purple explode high above me, the color of irises, so large that the bottom of the firework ends up in the hills. There are hearts floating in the sky, deep red, with garlands of silver around them. Streams of gold diamonds create lilies against the star-studded heavens, their tips touched with deep blue, purple, and red. Strawberries—I swear it—deep red with green leaves, brighten the hills. The finale goes on for ten minutes. The air above Florence is suffused with smoke, color, and noise. Some of the sounds are thunderous and deep. The boom of the fireworks' explosions, echoing off of hills and buildings, are reminders of San Giovanni's (St. John's) protection of this city during centuries of conflict.

All cities have their own ways of celebrating. Florence puts on a fine spectacle. In the United States fireworks usually brighten the skies above Fourth of July celebrations. As I sit high above the Arno, these fireworks become my Fourth. Amidst the "Oohing" and "Ahhing" that goes on is a unity of common joy, and long after the final burst of color has fled the sky, the scent of San Giovanni's colorful send off still falls across the city. The crowds dwindle, flowing east and west along the river, across the bridges and on to their homes. At dawn the people of Florence awaken to another year, hoping for the continued benediction of their Patron Saint.

Voices of Children

EARLY JULY IN FLORENCE AND THE CITY IS FULL of visitors.

Small handbills mark telephone posts throughout the city. On a wall near my apartment I read about the "VI Tuscany International Children's Chorus Festival." It is to be held on the evening of July 7 in a church across the city from my apartment.

The Basilica of San Lorenzo was the family church of the Medici family. In 1419 Brunelleschi, who was to design the dome of the great Duomo of Florence, oversaw the rebuilding of the church. It is located a short walk beyond the Duomo and Baptistry, in the center of Florence.

By 9:00 P.M., the scheduled start of the concert, I am comfortably seated inside. The spare simplicity of the space is overpowering. Columns fifty feet in diameter support a ceiling covered in gold leaf, centered on the Coat of Arms of the Medici. This was Cosimo's church, the one he patronized and financially supported. The old sacristy was the initial resting place of Cosimo and his son until they were moved to the Medici Chapel in the 1500s.

Suddenly the floor trembles and organ pipes cry out overhead as the voices of 450 children are raised in song. This evening's concert celebrates the music of Italy with fifteen children's choirs from Australia, the United States, Africa, South America, and Europe. An orchestra from the United Kingdom accompanies them in song. The choir begins to sing a beautiful piece from Mozart's *Requiem Mass* and my attention is drawn to the bronze pulpits.

These works, completed in 1465, are counted among Donatello's greatest achievements. The designs on the pulpits depict the passion, burial, and resurrection of Christ. The power of the scene of Christ's deposition from the cross is haunting, wrapped as it is in this particular music. The body of Christ, comforted by Mary Magdalene and his mother, and the grief on the faces of the many gathered around, are nearly photographic in their realism.

As the choir begins another song a small boy walks by, dressed in a white shirt and shorts, carrying an iridescent white balloon. As the child moves past me he releases the balloon. It floats up inside the nave. He quietly stares as it rises, transfixed perhaps by its slow, steady movement and the sound of such music. My eyes are drawn back to the pulpit, to the panel depicting Christ's ascension to heaven. Christ moves up and away from those gathered round him, their raised faces and hands all urge him to stay or to take them with him.

The church trembles underfoot as the children sing their last piece, a famous English Hymn entitled "Jerusalem." Most people know it as the hymn sung at the conclusion of the film *Chariots of Fire*. As the attendees express their appreciation in thunderous applause, I watch the small white balloon disappear into the expanse of the immense dome. We disperse for the evening. I head back towards the river, my mind replaying the glorious music.

A few couples wander, aimlessly, along the main street that connects the San Lorenzo with the Ponte Vecchio. The full moon is high in the sky, and blue shadows fall behind me as I make my way along ancient streets. The piazza in front of the Duomo is nearly empty. I stop for a few moments and take in the vast façade of the cathedral, suffused by the bright, blue-tinged luminescence of the moon. It is so beautiful. I have wanted to attend mass since arriving in Florence, and make a promise that tomorrow is the day.

Heartbeat

WHEN I ENTER SANTA MARIA DEL FIORE, THE DUOMO, on this Sunday morning, there are few people in the church. The organ music plays as I take a seat on the last row of benches. The music moves, slowly, almost methodically, out across the altar, wrapping its sound around the base of columns built nearly 600 years ago. It continues to rise as more people enter the cathedral. Soon the music fills the church. The floor vibrates as I lift my eyes up, up, up into the dome that only Brunelleschi believed could be built.

What history this place has seen: Savanarola, a medieval religious fundamentalist leader of the city, filled this church with his sermons, hypnotizing the people of Florence with his thunderous voice and terrifying prophecies; Black Plague surreptitiously and methodically fingered its way around these stones; ordination of cardinals and popes took place here, as well as funerals of the famous. Wars too numerous to recount have threatened its very existence. Yet it survived.

The music brings me back to the scene.

The Cardinal of Florence and other celebrants of the mass ascend the high altar. The organist presses the keys in one last thunderous, earth-shattering chord. I start counting: five seconds, ten seconds—fainter yet still alive—fifteen seconds, and then the organ's echoes are gone.

Silence.

The area now covered by Brunelleschi's dome was originally left open to the elements. One of the gifts he bestowed upon this place of worship, by designing and building the dome, was that of its echoes; they bind the space together. The mass and music are man's gift to each other and to this cathedral. The echo is the cathedral's voice saying: *I hear you. I'm absorbing your music and words into stone, wood, and art. The echo is the voice of my soul, a gift given back to you.* At the conclusion of the mass, the procession of celebrants weaves it way back to the sacristy. In the quiet that follows the final notes of music, I leave.

This great Duomo of Florence will always be a living thing, a place containing the growing good of men and women, a place of retreat and reflection. As I make my way over to a neighborhood café for lunch, a recent conversation with a friend comes back to me. We had been talking about how strongly many people feel about the city.

"Ah," he said, "Florence has a heartbeat. Sometimes you can hear it at the height of the day, and some days not at all. Her heart beats beneath these stone covered streets. Its deep pulse runs its course throughout every building standing in this valley. She is listening. She hears, she remembers, this pinnacled, church-towered, oft-flooded place I call home."

"Remember," he concluded, "as you walk her streets, meet her people, try as you might to become one with her, she will only allow in those who can hear the calming, murmured drum of her heart."

As I think back to the mass, and the echoes, I begin to believe that I have finally heard Florence's heartbeat.

She Lost Her Soul

THE FLOODS THAT CAME TO FLORENCE ON TWO DARK and nightmarish days in early November 1966 forever changed this city. The ravaging, oil-tainted water tore at treasures millennium old, ripped the paint off the beloved *Crucifixion* of Cimabue, and polluted countless homes, hearths, treasures, and monuments. The world descended on Florence to help her in a time of great peril. Art restoration, as a science, was reborn, and the Florentines rediscovered a heart they had forgotten.

I was talking to another friend this past week. We met at the Café Arno, just down the street from my apartment, and were enjoying an espresso.

"Florence is changed," he said. "She lost her soul after the floods."

How, I wondered, could a city so full of such generous people, and such beautiful art, have lost her soul? I asked him why he felt that way.

"Many of the businesses that made Florence unique never came back. The shop owners were our native mothers, fathers, and sons, and their generations past. Each of them carried with them a pride in quality and craftsmanship. Now on the streets in our city there are businesses like every other city in the world. You don't find the numerous fine, small shops and craftsmen like you used to; a few yes, but not like it used to be. The flood washed them from the city and they are gone forever. Businesses now move in and out along every major street here, some lasting only a few months or years, only to be replaced by another modern shop. They have no soul, no heart! So it goes."

He thought for a moment.

"Yes," he said, "I think that Florence lost her soul that November. She will be different, now, forever."

We sipped our espressos as I shared some stories about why I don't believe the city has lost her soul in any way.

"I was sitting at a café at Piazza della Repubblica a few days ago and noticed a flock of pigeons pecking away at a hard crust of bread that someone had tossed to them. I watched as they tried and tried to break off some small piece of the food."

"What do birds have to do with the soul of a city?" he shrugged.

"An elderly man sitting near me had been watching the birds as well," I continued. "He rose from his seat, walked over to the crust of bread, and smashed it with his shoe. As he was walking back to his chair, he said 'There. Now they can all eat.'" I awaited a reaction from my friend. Again he shrugged his shoulders.

"What else?"

"The other day," I began, "a young man, wearing black jeans and a billowy black shirt was walking down the street. He passed by me. In his hands were three small red-wrapped boxes, held intently, purposefully. His head was lowered as he made his nervous way down the street, his quick pace and energy apparent in staccato steps. As he neared a corner, one of the gift-wrapped boxes, a small one, fell out of his arms. It was something that he didn't seem to notice. Before I could call out, a young woman appeared from the shop just behind him. She called out for him to stop. He turned and graciously accepted the box before heading back down the street. He turned a corner, moved into a shadowed alley, and was gone."

"Yes, yes?" my friend responded.

"I walked up to her and said that I wondered where he was going. What were those cherished gifts carried with such care on a late Saturday afternoon in a dozing, peaceful, Florence? Will those gifts be remembered days or years from now? Will he remember the other gift his youthful energy inspired, or the generous gesture of a young woman on this side of the Arno?"

"You see," she answered, "it does not matter to me. But in his life, whatever they were, they matter. That is what is important, not possession, but love."

My friend smiled, lifted the small cup to his lips, and finished his espresso. "Perhaps I am wrong." He signaled the waiter to bring two more espressos. "Perhaps it is I who lost his soul. It is you who teaches me that the soul of Florence is still very much alive. Thank you."

Of all of the many memories that this season holds, this is one that shall, for certain, never leave me; the day the city's soul reclaimed one of its own.

Piazza Bench: July Afternoon

PIAZZA DELLA REPUBBLICA OCCUPIES THE GEOGRAPHIC heart of Florence. It lies along the great public promenade that connects the Ponte Vecchio and the Duomo. Not unlike the piazza surrounding the Duomo, this splendid square appears unexpectedly. The Mercato Vecchio (old market) once occupied this area of the city.

In the late 1800s, Florence was selected to be the new capital of a newly-unified Italy. In response, the city began an aggressive building campaign. A huge archway and office buildings were built along the western limit of what is now the Piazza della Repubblica. Three famous Florentine cafés, the Gilli, Giubbe Rosa, and Paszkowski, face out into the square. It is a beautiful, open, space.

The walk from my apartment to the Piazza usually takes about ten minutes and I find, more and more, that I am drawn to it in the afternoon, when the shade from the buildings provide welcome relief from the mid-July heat.

On this particularly hot afternoon I've been watching the few birds that dare come out in such heat—one bird in particular. A sparrow struggles, tries to fly, and simply hasn't the energy. She walks a few steps, looks around, flaps her wings, and then sits, the margins of her efforts penned in by the measured movement of shadow across stone. She edges forward after a few minutes, stretches her wings, then sits. Her bright eyes and clean feathers betray no illness. She simply seeks cooling shade.

If there were a way to join her I would do so. Eventually she takes to the sky and seeks the shadowed coolness of the large archway.

An old bench, with an area map of the city next to it, sits in front of the café. They both attract my attention. As it nears 4:00 P.M. I decide to note my observations of the many comings and goings in this most public of spaces.

4:00PM

A couple arrives at the bench; the woman wears too-tight, ochre colored jeans. The man sits cross-legged in dark brown slacks and stares up at COIN, one of the local department stores. An older Italian woman walks up to study the group on the bench, and then moves on. Two young girls sit and catch their breath while they watch several groups stroll by. Within minutes, they all leave.

4:15PM

A young couple arrives dressed up for dinner, she in black shift with golden arm bag, he in black flip-flops, gray slacks. She asks a woman if she will take a photo of them. She says yes. They smile. She takes, they wave a thanks, and part. Two women approach the map next to the bench, move, look, point, look, begin to move, look again, point, and move on. A couple follows them, she waving madly across the map, he, arms crossed, leans against the map and shrugs. They leave. The waists of two heavy tourists appear below the map. They stand, turn, stand, look, stand, turn, point. Stray fingers appear to the right of the map, and then they leave.

4:30PM

The bench is empty. A few strolling couples stop to stare at a CAUTION triangle someone placed nearby, then stroll on.

4:40PM

The bench remains empty. The base of four concrete roundels supports a solid gray marble top approximately twelve feet long. It is bowed in the center, and the supports on the outside barely touch the raised underside of the top. It looks weighted down by the history of over 130 years. Here it sits, day in, night long, awaiting its intended purpose, lonely or crowded, hot or cold, wet or dry.

Activity. The legs and lower bodies of two tourists approach the far side of the map. Weight shifts, arms' shadows seem to touch the map, darting back and forth across the dark stones of the square. Feet move. They turn, and are gone. Four feet appear now, a child and an adult, both sandaled. They spend a moment at the map and then bounce away.

4:45PM

A shadow from the arch moves steadily and stealthily across the square. Within the past thirty minutes, the shadow appears to have moved more than thirty feet. Two women arrive and sit, pull off their sandals and, crossing their feet, begin to talk. They reposition their feet and stare into nothingness, their soothing self-foot massage relieving tensions and fatigue. An older man on a bicycle, with a t-shirt turban-wrapped head, circles the plaza screaming like Tarzan. Bags and bags of white plastic hang from the handlebars. He circles three times, flails his arms in a wave, screams "Ciao" and disappears through the arch, a jean-jacketed, apocalyptic horseman of July's heat. While a young Italian strolls by the bench, chatting away on a cell phone, a group of Boy Scouts pauses at the map to study where they are and where they wish to go. The sound of the bells in the Campanile (bell tower) near the Duomo fills the air. Other bells, from other churches, join in. Clouds begin to fill the sky; perhaps a welcome shower is on the way. It is 5 P.M. Time to head home to prepare for the evening. I pay my check and slowly walk across the square.

I glance back at the bench before turning down the street. It occurs to me that pauses are what piazzas are really for. They mark our place within the city as we explore, meet, or celebrate; they provide a cooling retreat in the early and late passing of the day; they keep us headed in the right direction. So it is in Piazza della Repubblica on this summer evening. Celebrations, fatigue, the shared secrets of friends, and the conversations of strangers all meld into the warped backbone of an ancient bench.

Mystery

AS I MAKE MY WAY ALONG THE LUNGARNO TORRIGIANI, a street that passes in front of my apartment building, I happen to glance down at the river. A high wall traces both sides of the Arno through the city, and along the shore there is sand and debris. There is movement in the brush below me. A head appears. What I perceive to be the head of a beaver pokes out of the undergrowth. I watch as a large, brown, furry body emerges, (Surely a beaver!) followed by a long round tail.

That's the biggest rat I've ever seen, I think.

Easily as large as a terrier, it slogs through the mud and makes its way into the river. It begins to swim away. The entrance to my building is across the street. I rush over to ask the all-knowing Signor Bachi, the doorman.

"Signor Bachi," I say. "I can't believe what I just saw in the river!"

"What?" he asks. His eyes grow wider, his hands move more emphatically. "What?"

"I don't know the word in Italian. It was the size of a small dog," I said, stumbling through my Italian. "It was brown and . . ."

"Oh, you saw a small dog in the river?" he interrupts.

"No, no, not a dog, it looked like a dog, but it was brown, and had a round tail and . . ."

"I see dogs along the river all the time." His face takes on a puzzled look. "You saw a small dog with a round tail?" Confusion clearly shows on his face.

"No, I'm sorry Signor Bachi. My bad Italian! I don't know the word. A rat."

"Rata?" he replies. "You saw a rata? What's a rata?"

My frustration is starting to show. I simply don't know the word in Italian. Thunder booms across the city. We are in for a much welcome rain.

"Mmmm . . . let's see," I say. "Ok. Brown. Large. Round tail. Swims. River Arno."

His eyes squint in concentration. They became slits, the pupils barely visible. His hand comes up to his mouth and he shifts his weight.

A flash of lightening strikes a building across the river. Gusts of wind blow into the lobby of the building.

"Ah," he jumps.

I jump.

"What?" I reply.

"The big 'rata'. It's a coypu, a kind of rodent that lives all over Italy. You'll see them a lot in the rivers."

"Ah, I see." Another loud sound of thunder reminds me that I have clothes drying out on my terrace. "Ok. Thank you, Signor Bachi, for solving the mystery."

"It's nothing," he replied.

I wave goodbye and head for the elevator.

Coypu my eye, I think. *That was the biggest "rata" I've ever seen.*

I use my large terrace for everything: sunbathing, drying clothes, eating breakfast or dinner, and sometimes just sitting to enjoy a glass of wine. I rush out to pick up clothes that have spent the day drying in the Tuscan heat.

Great gusts of energy fly around the flowers and bang windows across the city; the sound of shattered glass is a reminder of the approaching storm's strength. The black curtain of clouds moves swiftly; bright bolts of electricity touch the earth followed by a loud, ear-shattering cry. Streaks of lightening move horizontally over my head, and vertical shocks strike the hills all around.

Large drops of cool rain begin to pattern the terrace, quickly becoming a large domino game before the sky pours forth. Bright bursts of electricity flash. More windows bang shut, dogs howl, trees bend, and flowers snap their stems. The rain comes in heavy sheets, pounding the terrace and creating a curtain of waterfalls that flows off the roof.

Down it comes, and in the course of its hour of passing, it washes away the dirt of the day; broken glass, sweat, and the long-forgotten detritus of the people flow down into the streets, into the river, and on to the sea. The cooling breeze that follows the storm is very welcome. As I go about preparing dinner, I think about the much-anticipated visit of a friend from California. She will be staying at a stunner of a hotel that is perched high on a hill above the city, the Torre di Bellosguardo.

Fireflies
(For Barbara)

THE TORRE DI BELLOSGUARDO (TOWER OF BEAUTIFUL View, or, more literally, Tower of Beautiful Outlook) rests on a high hill overlooking Florence. A friend of Dante, Guido Cavalcanti, is said to have built his home and a tower on this site. A villa was later built around that house and tower. In 1913, the widow of Baron Giorgio Franchetti, Baroness Marion Hornstein, bought the villa and, until 1948, made it into a place of retreat for a privileged few. Its current life, as an exclusive hotel, invites guests to stay amidst incredible surroundings. My friend has arrived and has invited me to join her for drinks. It is a moonless night. I drive up to the hotel.

Imagine a night so black that you cannot see a hand in front of your face, a night that surrounds you in scented garden air and wraps you in a timeless haze. A bat joins me, flying just ahead of the car's headlights as I drive up a harrowing, narrow road and enter the graveled driveway of Bellosguardo. Each time I approach this villa, through the cypress-lined drive, I am reminded of lines from Elizabeth Barrett Browning's poem, "Aura Leigh":

I found a house, at Florence, on the hill
Of Bellosguardo. 'Tis a tower that keeps
A post of double observation o'er
The valley of Arno . . . straight toward Fiesole
And Mount Morello and the setting sun,
The Vallombrosan mountains to the right,
Which sunrise fills as full as crystal cups
Wine-filled . . . Beautiful.
The city lay along the ample vale,
Cathedral, tower and palace, piazza and street;
The river trailing like a silver cord
Through all, and curling loosely, both before,
And after . . .

My friend greets me at the main entry. After a long and wonderful conversation we leave the hotel for a stroll outside.

The gardens here have been lovingly tended for over two centuries. The result is a place full of spectacular colors and scents. Large cypresses surround a manicured lawn. A beguiling bed of roses, trellised so that each arch is a different color, leads to a water garden that weaves along the top of a high wall with views over Florence. A stone seat, with scented climbers on each side, provides an unobstructed view of the city. On a night like this, the garden's dark paths invite mystery and magic.

We pause at the entrance, a pathway protected on either side by fifteen-foot-high hedgerows. As we begin to stroll into the enwrapping darkness, there is a sparkle of light, then another. Into the midst of blackness, from within the hedges, comes a breathtaking profusion of fireflies. Their yellow-diamond incandescence illuminates the night. A cloud of iridescence surrounds us. Some fireflies light our way from within the deep recesses of the hedgerows. Others remain closely by our side, accompanying our slow and steady pace along the path. Splashes from the nearby water garden accompany the light. The scent of roses surrounds us as we arrive at the far end of the hedgerows. Mesmerized by our good fortune, we are speechless for a few moments. When we turn around, the cloud of fireflies retreats back up the pathway to await another visitor to this garden of infinite beauty perched high on a hill.

Giardino dei Semplici

MY FRIEND ONLY STAYED FOR A SHORT TIME AND, AS preparations are made for a two-week visit to Assisi, I make plans to visit a place in Florence I have not yet seen: the Giardino dei Semplici. The garden is hidden off of a side street not far from the Accademia, home to Michelangelo's *David*.

Semplici (literally, simples) refers to the raw ingredients that medieval apothecaries used to prepare medicines. A Medici, Grand Duke Cosimo I, had varied interests; one was research regarding the expanded use of such herbs for medicinal purposes. In 1545, Niccolo' Tribolo was commissioned to begin work on the garden's design and installation. With few exceptions, work has continued ever since. Many of the drugs we use today can trace their roots, literally, to this place.

The gates are usually open from 9 A.M. Monday-Friday and close at 1 P.M. I board a bus at the Bardi stop, near my apartment, at 9:10. The buses often sit for five to ten minutes while the driver takes a stroll, stretches his legs, or has a quick espresso at the local stand. This morning is no different and the driver returns at 9:15, starts up the engine, and we're off. The buses that run in the city's historic center are electric, very small, bright orange, and only seat eight.

We cross the river on the Ponte alle Grazie (bridge of thanks) and are almost immediately plunged into the semi-darkness that characterizes the maze of narrow streets in the old city center. As we near the Piazza Salmevi, two very well dressed older women board. A young man and I immediately get up to offer our seats to the ladies. One of the manners that is so imbued in Italian society is courtesy and deference to older people. Standing for them is simply something that is done, something expected.

The bus makes it way north, past the church of Santa Croce. From there, we head west past the Tempio Isaelitico (Florence's only Jewish temple), and then north, again, past the Accademia (The line!). We finally arrive at the Convent and Piazza of San Marco. The entire trip takes only ten minutes. I leave the bus here and head northeast along the Via Giorgio La Pira to the Giardino dei Semplici.

As I approach the gate, I find it locked. I check the sign and it confirms the hours are LUNEDI (MONDAY) A VENERDI (FRIDAY) 0900-1300. I check for other entrances, see none, and approach a man working inside the fence.

"Where is the entrance to the garden? This gate is locked."

"Oh." He looks up sheepishly, wearing a San Francisco 49ers cap. "Today we're closed. We have to water the garden."

"Ah." I nod. I wonder why it would be closed for watering. "Monday, then?"

"Well, I think we will be open Monday. We should be."

"Should I call before I come over?"

He puts an arm out and leans against a nearby tree. His face tightens in concentration. "The person who usually staffs the phone is out, so I don't think that anyone will answer."

I smile and thank him for his trouble. As I walk back toward the Academia I decide to try again, after my return from Assisi. I take a seat at a nearby bus stop, shake my head, and wonder if Grand Duke Cosimo I ever had this much difficulty getting in.

The bus stop bench is empty as I take a seat. The Piazza San Marco, another of Florence's beautiful public places, is a hive of activity. Mopeds and cars swirl around the center of the plaza. City and tour busses dart onto and off of side streets, appearing almost as quickly as they disappear. The façade of the Convent and Church of San Marco stand along one side of the piazza. I am only steps from the Accademia, a five-minute walk north from the Duomo, yet the day to day coming and going of locals is more evident here than in the more well known corners of the city center.

A young woman with a briefcase climbs the ancient steps of a building and enters. The fruit stand, across from where I sit, is crowded with business-suited men and women, all vying for some of the succulent, fresh produce. There are two older men, wearing hats, sitting in concentration over a chessboard. A few horns sound; a few greetings between friends rise above the general buzz and hum of the streets.

Tomorrow I leave for Assisi to participate in a two-week writing workshop. As I take in this square, and the cacophony around me, I wonder what quiet the heart of Umbria might offer. A bus arrives and, as I board, I make the decision to visit a recently discovered retreat, hidden within the Boboli Gardens across the city. The heat is rising, and the high reaches of the Boboli beckon.

The bus rumbles down cobblestoned streets, narrowly misses a few errant tourists, and twists around the oldest part of the city. We cross the river on the Ponte Santa Trinita, a bridge rebuilt to Michelangelo's original design after it was destroyed during the Second World War. The bright sun glares down. I leave the bus a few steps from the Pitti Palace, a short walk from the Ponte Vecchio, enter the gardens, and walk up towards the great Fortress of Belvedere.

Near the top of the Boboli Gardens, close to the high wall ending the protective bastions of Renaissance Florence, is a coffeehouse built in 1776 as a retreat for one of the leading families of the Republic. It is now a public café-restaurant and, even at 10:30 in the morning, offers welcome quiet from the noise of the city.

Beneath fifteen huge, bright white umbrellas, there are twenty small tables. There are only four other visitors seated near the back of the café. The waiter takes my order and leaves me to gaze down over the city. This side of the Arno river is known as the *Altrarno* (the other side of the Arno). The gardens flow beneath the café toward the Pitti Palace. I can see the nearby Church of Santo Spirito framed by a tapestry of trees and houses. Across the river, the massive dome of the Duomo, the multi-colored spire of the Campanile and the smaller dome above the Baptistry rise above the sea of Tuscan-red rooftops. They shimmer against the heat and blue sky.

Off in the western distance the mountains of the Alpi Apuane, towards Montecatini Terme and Carrara, are a far off blue-hazed vision. There is an occasional breeze that flutters the umbrellas, and sparrows hop nearby seeking a longed for scrap of bread, some finding a treasure in the dust. The small breakfast I have ordered arrives. The sound of cups placed on saucers, an occasional placement of a spoon on china, and the muted conversation of the customers and waiters rustle underneath the white canopy. I finish my cappuccino and request an espresso from the waiter. He arrives with the tiny cup.

Espresso: a black, acidic, magical brew; the foam on its surface and the dark circles of coffee deep inside the cup are an invitation to enter in, to enjoy, to taste. Mixed in with this wonderful taste is the gauzed texture of cigarette smoke. The late-morning sun has slightly occluded the tendrils that rise, catch the breeze, and move across the tablecloths. They mix with the deep exotic scent of espresso, reminding me of how transient such moments are. In their pause, they magnify the everyday and create memories carried for a lifetime.

I spend an hour writing, or taking in the extraordinary view, and eventually pay the waiter.

This is the side of Florence so few see. The piazzas at the Duomo, San Marco, the Signoria, are all crowded and hot. Here, in the hills above the Altrarno and the Pitti Palace lies a gem of a retreat, where an espresso and a small meal can be enjoyed amidst the breeze, the sounds of birds, and the murmur of other appreciative visitors. The long, languid hours passed in such places add so much to the Florentine experience.

Tomorrow will be a full day; first, a noon departure from Florence and three hours on a train, then the beginning of what I hope to be a two-week period of creative enrichment with other writers. As I walk back down the terraced hillside and leave the garden, my heart is full of anticipation of what lies ahead in Assisi.

Umbria

Umbrian Train

I AM HEADED TO ASSISI. AFTER ALMOST TWO MONTHS in Florence the opportunity to join other writers, in the heart of Umbria, will be a welcome change. Umbria rests between two mountain ranges in the very heart of Italy. The trip will take me southeast out of Florence, through Tuscany, and on to Assisi.

The main train station in Florence, Santa Maria Novella, is a whirl of activity: Eurostars dethrone first class traveling tourists; regional trains head to Viareggio, Borgo San Lorenzo, and the coasts; intercity trains that crisscross Europe come and go. The sun is nearly overhead, and I seek the welcome shade of a track platform to eat a small sandwich and drink some water. My train pulls in. I board, settle into a comfortable seat, lean back, and let Umbria come to me.

The train route is generally north out of Florence, and then, after a five-minute transit through a tunnel, out to the south towards Arezzo. From Arezzo, the train will head to Cortona, the last large Tuscan town I will see before entering Umbria. From there it will travel on to Perugia, and finally, Santa Maria degli Angeli, the station for Assisi.

The countryside flashes by as tunnels of deep green give way to the gray granite walls of overpasses. Along the way we cross the A1 Autostrada to Rome and the countryside widens. There are vast fields of corn, vineyards, and sunflowers. We stop often. In the Terranuova Station I notice a mosaic along the main platform. It proclaims: *La Ferroviari e la vita de la Popolo* (The railroad is the life of the people). It makes me think of World War II, or before, when Italy was consumed by political earthquakes that shook the world.

The fields below Cortona are blanketed with sunflowers. The word for sunflowers in Italian, *girasole*, literally translates to "sunflower," however, many people interpret the word as "turning to the sun." As far as I can see, on both sides of the train, are vibrant bright yellow and green flowers. A few of their faces bow to the inevitable harvest; it is already too late to catch some in full bloom.

A lone sentinel, the church of Santa Maria delle Grazie stands above the valley outside the city walls near Cortona. The old city thrusts itself up along a mountainside, towers and walls all gray-white in the sun. Cortona's train station, located in the valley below the old town, is post-war plain. As the train pulls out of the station, I notice two young men who share the platform laughing with each other about some private joy.

Lake Trasimeno comes into view. It seems only fitting that a heart-shaped lake should be the first sign that we have entered Umbria. Small villas and parks dot the nearby shoreline. Hills rise in the lavender-hazed distance beyond the lake. Villas, towers, and small villages blink past us as we approach Perugia.

Perugia, the largest city in Umbria, is home of the Umbrian Museum of Art and a world-renowned jazz festival. As the train pulls to a stop in the station, posters announce that the festival is underway. Numerous passengers disembark and greet friends from Germany, Italy, and the U.S. When we are only a few minutes outside of Perugia I suddenly see Assisi off in the distance.

It rises well above the floor of this valley, radiantly white, with towers and roofs sparkling in the sun. The Basilica of St. Francis and the domes of other churches thrust themselves up above the ancient walls of the city. We arrive in Santa Maria Degli Angeli, the Assisi train station, and I'm soon in a taxi headed up to the Hotel Giotto, my home for the next two weeks. The taxi driver is a kind, older man who flatters my Italian and offers to arrange a tour of some of the towns in the area. For now, it is more than enough just to recall this dream of a train ride through the hills of southern Tuscany into the heart of Umbria. After the formalities of check-in, I go up to my room to unpack. The floor-to-ceiling shutters are open. I walk over to the balcony and take in the view.

Trees. I shall always remember the trees.

Cypresses surround a small church garden directly below the windows of my room. Birch, oak, and umbrella pines march upwards to the left. A hill carpeted with olive trees stretches down below the city walls to a valley of late-summer green. An alley of poplar, fresh from a Monet painting, stands far off. A town across the valley stands out above fields of rolled, golden hay, and fields the color of Cordovan leather reach up to touch it, holding it suspended. Mountains march high against the horizon; their hazy blue summits pierce the aquamarine sky. Cars crisscross the roads down in the valley, unheard. A single train's whistle cries out as it glides through the towns below, and villas of every imaginable color dot the landscape. Here and there, a bell tower heralds a church or town.

What is it, travelers have asked for ages, *about Italy?* For those whose ancestors came from these valleys, from this country, the answer probably lies in their lineage. For the rest of us, the answer simply lies in the timeless view of verdant abundance below room twenty-four. I change for dinner and go down to the lobby.

After ordering a cooling drink at the bar, I wander out onto the terrace. Evening approaches. Shadows lengthen in the far away towns and fields, and a few bells announce the evening mass. I rest for an hour before dinner, with reflections of a day full of wonder still fresh in my mind.

Piazza del Commune

NOON. THE PIAZZA COMMUNE IN ASSISI IS ALIVE WITH
bells. A dog across the square howls in off-key accompani-
ment. An interesting parade moves through here today. An
army of young tourists passes by, sandaled and Nike-d,
wearing tight leggings and shorts, some licking ice cream
cones, others buried deep in conversation, still others biting
nails and listening to the shared secrets of youth. They move
to the center of the Piazza and stand for a few moments,
taking in a guide's overview of the place.

A behemoth of a woman in a tank top and shorts
wobbles through the square, followed by an equally satiated
man. They find themselves walking in the shadows of church
gargoyles, and they become living grotesques in their own
right. A tiny car, deep marine-blue, glides through, the driver
talking away on his cell phone—here, in front of a temple
dedicated in 239 A.D.

The cafés are beginning to fill up for lunch hour; the
shade of a large umbrella gives welcome respite from an
increasingly hot late-July sun. A postal truck, an "Espresso
Courier" (bright red and unexpected), and a small white
Fiat from the Commune Assisi drive by. Throngs of

backpack-shouldered tourists and baseball-capped elders tromp through the Piazza following a guide with a flag. Several monks appear to float across the square. Their ample brown robes billow in the breeze behind them. Assisi is a physical city, and each tourist who walks by seems wrapped in a mist of sweat and strain. They gaze into cafés, wondering, by their gap-jawed stare, if they will find rest, a cool drink, and a good meal within.

The Piazza Communale has witnessed the construction of Roman temples, the arrival of St. Francis, the rise of Christianity, the ebb and flow of pilgrims, and the slow and steady pace of progress. So much history contained within one place! High on this hill in Umbria, in a piazza centered in Assisi, is where the passage of people and time becomes a haze, our common link to centuries of ancestors captured by the wind as we pass by, tossed into the tower-stabbed lapis-blue sky.

Places of Light

THE WOOD-COVERED HILLS OF MONTE SUBASIO, ABOVE Assisi, were well known to Saint Francis. Before our class meets each day, there is time to explore the many paths that cross the mountain. The fresh air and cooling shadows of the forest offer welcome privacy from the city below. I spend a part of each day in the high reaches of the hills. As I approach the intersection of two paths, I stop to take in the view.

Trees on each side of the trail gather closer overhead and rise to a meeting point, creating an archway. The shade-dappled path leads up into a nave as light, filtering through the trees, takes on the colors of stained-glass windows. The sun pierces through the pine-scented haze of woodland air; its rays fall on the dusty, earthen floor. Birds move back and forth across the path, their music filling the air.

I turn and walk back down the lane towards town and pass a few others who quietly wander across the mountain. We all seem to share the same appreciation of the quiet and splendor around us. It is afternoon when I approach the city ramparts. I reenter the town through the Porta Perlici, the only gate on the northern expanse of the ancient city wall. I turn down a side lane, head west towards the Basilica of St. Francis. The massive façade of the church is spectacular. A huge rose window is centered above two mammoth wooden doors. A large bell tower stands out against the deepening blue of the afternoon sky. A small crowd stands at the main entrance.

Construction of the cathedral started in 1228, a mere two years after the death of St. Francis. The lower basilica was completed in two years and now houses the remains of the Saint, along with an astonishing array of medieval works of art. During the fourteenth and fifteenth centuries Giotto painted the frescoes in the Madonna Chapel, Simone Martini painted the interior of the chapel of St. Martin, and Pietro Lorenzetti frescoed the left side of the transept in the lower church. It is Lorenzetti's work that brings me here this afternoon.

She resides deep within the lower church in the Basilica of St. Francis of Assisi, painted over 750 years ago by Lorenzetti; *Madonna with St. Francis and St. John the Evangelist*, lovingly called the *Sunset Madonna*. It is said that a mysterious glow suffuses the fresco at sunset. I sit patiently and wait for the moment to arrive.

As the sun sinks ever lower in the sky, a bright beam of light enters through an open door behind me and begins to inch its way across the wall. Slowly, the illumination moves across the fresco. Details leap from the art: the path of the brush across a hand; the thin ridge of violet that separates a cloak from Mary's earthen-colored face; the touch of her hand on the infant; a grain of gold. The child's face glows. The Madonna's halo reflects golden light out onto the warbled floor of this ancient church. The illumination lasts for only a few moments and then, as suddenly as it arrived, the shaft of light is gone.

It is difficult to leave. I wonder what other furtive secrets this cathedral full of visions must hold. In a few minutes this sacred space will fill up with those who wish to share in the mass. I rise and go. This *Sunset Madonna* will stay with me, rest in my heart. Even today I can see her smile floating above the polished skin of worn tiles within that place of miracles and faith.

Marionettes

THE ANCIENT CHURCH OF SAN STEFANO LIES, NEARLY hidden, along a tiny lane in the center of Assisi. If you aren't watching, you'll miss it. The discovery the church, and the marionettes, was unexpected.

I walk down from the Piazza Communale in Assisi early on a particularly hot afternoon. The music of a Puccini aria greets me as I round the corner of a dark alleyway. Two women sit in the cool shadow of an old building. They seem to stare into their past, transfixed by the music, remembering times with family and loved ones. The music leads me to the door of the now deconsecrated church. The outer doors to the sanctuary are open, and the inner glass doors are bolted shut.

There are several women sitting in the church. In the space where the altar used to be is a concert grand piano, and a woman stands beside it. As she sings I watch and listen to a few minutes of this master class. My eyes are drawn up to the walls of the church. On the right side of the nave, well above the pews, are twelve open-fronted, box-like containers. Hanging within each is a marionette. Their names are etched on the edges of the bins: St. Francis, Young;

St. Francis, Old; Santa Chiara; Friar; and many more. Each figure has been carved with great care and with attention to fine details of eyes, nose, cheekbone, and hand. I study them for some time, unable to imagine their purpose, particularly in such a place. I leave during a pause in the singing. A small sign, near an archway, proclaims the presence of the Café Trovellesi.

Just inside the old stone archway lies a rose-filled courtyard. Long, thin iris leaves reach up, monuments to past spring glories. Four small green metal tables lean into a rough-hewn stone terrace. There is an unobstructed view, at the precipice, out over the wide Umbrian valley. Potted geraniums and fresh herbs line the wall nearest my seat, and ancient pine trees curve overhead to frame the view.

An animated young woman appears, greets me, and shows me to a table. She is a raven-haired, blue-eyed stunner. We talk. I share my love for Assisi with her, and she her fascination with tourists who come and go in less than a day, never really seeing anything of the town. I think to ask her about the marionettes. As she brings a welcome bottle of water from the nearby bar, she unexpectedly shares their story.

Assisi used to sponsor a group of young people to perform a play about the life of St. Francis. From the time of her young adulthood—since age thirteen to be exact—she had been one of the members of the cast of puppeteers, Santa Chiara. For nearly twelve years these plays were produced and given in a large hall of the city's school, a setting that provided ample space, but not, as she said, " . . . a very religious setting," for the performance. About five years ago, interest waned in the play, and many of the people who had willingly participated in it were now on to other things. The performance had not been given since.

I order a light lunch from her and, while I wait for it to arrive, think about the circle of knowledge within the small towns of Italy. Had it not been for the voice of a soprano echoing down an alleyway, the church's glass doors being open to allow passersby to see inside, my studying the marionettes above the nave and then asking a stranger in a café what they could have possibly meant, I never would have come to know about the marionettes of Assisi.

Lunch arrives, a pepper-flocked snow of fresh mozzarella, deep red tomatoes, and fresh basil. A simple salad served in this quiet place. The light cuts clean through the trees of shade above my table, and the tablecloth is spotted with clear, round domino dots of light. Sparrows cross my view. Far down in the valley, sharp fingers of emerald-green cypresses cut against a golden fleece of long-since mowed hay. Even here, the relentless sun raises the scent of heated sheaves to my senses. In the distance, villas dot the rising foothills. They are places of my desire, of my dreams, with imagined wisteria-covered loggias that provide shade to private terraces. Secret. Quiet.

I settle my bill, thank her, and depart through the archway. I stand for a few moments to soak up this experience, to absorb it like breath, to carry it with me into others places and times. This town never ceases to astound me. It is a place of ups and downs and dreams on terraces laid out over the peace of Umbria.

I think often of those puppets honed from the wood of faith. They wait quietly above both doubters and believers, collecting dust and memories. A day will again arrive when they shall be brought back to life in the hands of others who love the story of St. Francis, who carry a unique heart-fired passion for theater, and a belief in the dreams of Geppetto. I hope that when the marionettes return to life someday, they will fill the halls of this ancient city with the timeless story of a saint who once walked amidst the forests from whence they came.

Treasures of Foligno

IN 1997, A MAJOR EARTHQUAKE SHOOK CENTRAL UMBRIA. Much of the world's attention was focused on the damaged frescoes in the upper nave of the Basilica of St. Francis in Assisi. However, the small town of Foligno was at the epicenter of the quake and sustained major damage. Many people know of Foligno from a video showing its oldest bell tower falling away into the church below. Since then the town has recovered from the majority of the damage.

Art Workshops International, the organization that planned this Writer's Workshop in Assisi, has made arrangements for a small group of us to visit Foligno so that we may view an incredible collection of fourteenth and fifteenth-century frescoes within the Palazzo Trinci.

The drive down into the valley to Foligno takes us past olive groves and ancient churches. The green mass of Monte Subasio remains on our left as we approach Spello, a town dating itself to Roman times. We arrive in Foligno about thirty minutes later. Once inside the Palazzo Trinci, our guide relates a brief history of the Trinci family. In 1310 the patriarch of the family, Rinaldo, received papal endorsement for ruling the town. Over time the family extended their rule to include many of the largest towns in central Umbria: Assisi, Spello, and Montefalco. This Palazzo was the family home until 1439, when the family fell out of papal favor. The frescoes we have come to see were commissioned to decorate many of the interior walls of the palace.

"Over the centuries, the frescoes had fallen into disrepair," the guide tells us. "The building was used as a courthouse and then a jail. For many years it remained empty. Ten years ago a restorer by the name of Romeo Seccamani began the daunting task of refurbishing all of the frescoes in the palace." She points to some of the walls in the main entry hall. "The results of his work are truly amazing.

"The two most famous artists to have worked here were Ottaviano Nelli (1370-1444) and Gentile da Fabriano (1370-1427). One of the largest rooms contains enormous representations of personages from the Bible and Roman history; another is 'The Hall of the Planets,' so called for its depictions of the seven planets then known—Mercury, Venus, Earth, Moon, Jupiter, Saturn, and the Sun. There are also frescoes celebrating the arts—Grammar, Music, Philosophy, Dialectic, Geometry, Arithmetic, Philosophy, and Rhetoric."

I approach a painting for a closer look. One of the steps involved in creating a fresco is the creation of what is called *senopia*. The term is derived from Sinope, a town on the Black Sea, where a rare red pigment was transformed into paint. The paint was used to draw the final design (cartoon) upon which the artist applied color. On many of the frescoes I see the outlines of the original senopia— something exceedingly rare.

The rooms are full of extraordinary work. Bright crimson reds and emerald greens shine from the walls. A chariot, pulled by four horses painted in dark auburn brown, leaps across a wall. Neptune peers down at me, his indigo toga looking as if it were painted only yesterday. The years of neglect have taken their toll on many of the works, and large sections of some frescoes are missing. Such is the case in the main hall where scenes of feudal battles are interrupted by masses of sand-colored fill, applied when the restorer could do no more.

The triumph within the Palazzo is the chapel where Nelli's *Life of the Virgin* radiates off of walls covered in gold, crimson, and navy blue. The room is approximately forty feet by forty feet, and over sixteen separate frescoes cover every inch of the four walls and ceiling. We stand in awe.

It seems somehow appropriate that in 1472 one of the first editions of Dante's *Divine Comedy* was printed in the nearby Palazzo Orfini. Standing in the midst of such glorious art, our guide reads aloud:

And I shall circle, Lady of Heaven, till home
Thou thy son follow into the sphere supreme
And make it more divine since thou art come.

As I listen to the words I imagine Dante envisioning such a place of splendor for heaven.

The frescoes of Palazzo Trinci are another of Italy's hidden treasures. It seems to me that Italians carry within their hearts an insatiable desire to care for their artistic heritage. Certainly there is the Sistine Chapel, the *Last Supper*, and the *Pieta*. In Foligno as well, is a treasure of unimaginable value that many Italians may never see. That doesn't seem to matter to them. What they most cherish is that the art exists, that it ties them to a great lineage of men and women whose works established Italy as the birthplace of the world's greatest masterpieces.

The bus winds along the road towards Assisi as vineyards and ancient walls flash by. I gaze out the window as we pass through one of the city gates and feel extremely grateful for a few hours spent amongst the treasures of Foligno.

Assisi Sunset

MY TIME IN ASSISI IS COMING TO A CLOSE. THE PAST weeks have been filled with wonderful experiences, and many friends have been made. The days have passed by far too quickly. It will be difficult to leave.

Evening settles upon the city as a group of friends join together on the terrace for dinner. The sky streaks pink and saffron. Hang gliders appear above us and float through the air. From somewhere high up on Mount Sebasio, above the hermitage of San Francesco, they become human butter-flies, and stretch their white, red, orange, and yellow wings above their bodies.

From the terrace we watch them, counting ten at a time. They pierce the sky as they descend slowly, some passing close to the village, then moving down to land softly in a mown hay field out in the valley. Others disappear behind church towers or trees to descend in hoped-for safety. They move at the pace of Umbria. One slow glide after another, they float through the evening sky and find rest in fields of browned and baled hay, softly protected by the ever-darkening wrap of this peaceful valley.

Church bells rise up from the expanse of green and gold below us, and the bells of Assisi reply. As sunset reddens the air, the light gives depth and texture to the roofs and walls below us.

The long shadows of towers and cypress trees cascade across the hillsides of this splendid town, and in the warm, rapturous air, I recall moments of magic: days of walking high in the forest arches surrounded by ethereal light that once kept St. Francis warm; the accidental discovery of marionettes secluded in corners of an ancient church; the surreal experience of standing on glass-covered floors suspended over Roman ruins; and the *Sunset Madonna*. Most special of all, however, are the moments spent on this terrace thrust out high above the city and valley. It has been here that the human bonds of affection have been strengthened.

Come the dark hours before dawn tomorrow, I have to leave, to move back into the world, away from this place of such physical strength and religious spirit. The night gathers ever more closely around our conversation and laughter. The final laps of light touch the far off hilltops across the valley, and we say our goodbyes. Deep in my heart resides the hope that I can hold these memories as clearly as I stand here this night.

It must now be enough to watch the lights flicker on in distant windows, to breathe deeply this Umbrian moon–thick air, and to prepare for the days ahead when such memories will bring me back to my beloved Assisi.

Intermission

FLORENCE.

The oppressive heat of early August hazes the valley. I make plans to visit another of Italy's treasures, a city afloat on the sea. My destination is a place so full of art, so wrapped in history, so blessed with beauty, that its very name evokes vivid visions of gondolas, Byzantine churches, canals, and cooling sapphire seas.

I am off to Venice.

Venezia

Eurostar to Venice

THE MAIN TRAIN STATION IN FLORENCE, SANTA MARIA Novella, stands in stark contrast to the church after which it is named. The station is a magnificent, open, well-lighted space. It was built in the mid 1930s and is a modern, chalky-tan marvel.

My trip to Venice today will only take about three hours. I board a "Eurostar," the fastest of Italian trains, a few minutes after it arrives in the station, and settle into a very comfortable red fabric-covered seat. The train hums, anxious for the tracks to shoulder its upcoming journey.

We depart Florence on time and are soon accelerating through the countryside northeast of the city. The Arno breathes past us at lightening speed. The train is drawn to Bologna, and we begin to head north of the Florentine valley, into the region known as Emilgila-Romagna. Olive groves flash by. The voice of the conductor announces, "Breakfast is available in car five." The train climbs into the verdant hills as the green haze outside the window blurs at vibrating speed. We enter numerous tunnels.

I fall under the spell of the Eurostar to Venice. Such trains these are! They slink into and out of ports of call, traversing thousands of years' history in a flash. The scale of Italy enables such trips—a quick journey to Venice for an afternoon, a day in Assisi, or a day in Rome.

The hill towns between Florence and Bologna are alpine-like. The balconies are alight with red, pink, and verdant green flowers. Comforters are draped easily over second-floor porches, and shutters have been opened to what must be fresh mountain air. The train will, from these heights, soon seek the open fields beyond Bologna and the fertile earth of the Veneto.

We approach Bologna. A friend recently told me that some of Italy's more modern apartment building design is referred to as *Brutalita* (brutality). The tall, monotonous buildings surrounding the area make it easy to understand the use of such a word. The station walls are a mass of graffiti. Metallic-gray train cars full of automobiles sit nearby, and their cargo is wrapped in a confusion of wire netting. Some passengers lean out of graffiti-laden windows in a train next to ours. Smoke rises from their lips; flicks of ashes are strewn onto the gravel like the seconds of their lives too soon lost. Their faces betray a desire to move aboard our streamlined Eurostar and let it take them far from where they have to go. I hope to return to visit the university and the other treasures for which Bologna is justifiably famous.

We sprint across the flatlands towards Padua, a large industrial city halfway between Bologna and Venice. This region of Italy is called the Veneto; cornfields, rice paddies, pear orchards, and vineyards flash by. It is very fertile land. The train approaches Mestre, the last stop before we cross the Venetian Lagoon to enter Venice.

The city of Mestre is now known for its growing population. Cost of living in Venice is such that many locals have moved away from the Lagoon islands, seeking homes in less expensive areas on the mainland. The station is a hive of activity.

Our train silently crosses the gray metal-webbed railway bridge connecting the mainland to Venice. Electric towers flash by the windows as automobiles move parallel to us on the Ponte Della Libertà, their own bridge. The city begins to make itself known, and there is a moment when I suddenly feel the interloper, intruding into someone else's dream. Spires and domes, with walls the color of honey, appear to float above a sparkling cerulean sea. There is a sense that we are being led inexorably into that dream, that there is no place we can go but to a vision floating in a lagoon.

We arrive.

Green. The water of the Grand Canal is green, liquid emerald, and clean. A sea-tainted breeze washes around me as I leave the station. The palazzos that front the canal are glorious—all filigree, red-brick based, stucco colored like the earth, deep ochre and russet brown. Green shutters, a deeper green than the water, protect windows from the direct midday sun, and the small side canals are packed with gondolas. My eyes, so full of the subtle beauty of Florence, squint into a sea-tinged haze of inexorable splendor.

Here water rules, not man nor Medici. The Canal's ebb and flow laps continuously, inevitably eating its way through the foundations of this floating city. The boats vary from freight-carrying, metal-clad tubs to private boats of stunning mahogany. Water taxis sweep by. Luggage-carrying gondolas vie for room among the maze of vessels in front of the station. I find a water taxi and tell the operator the name of my hotel.

We float down the Grand Canal. Palaces and towers, villas and restaurants, museums and parks all rise above the ever-present sea. The colors of maroon, blue, crimson red, ochre, and green weave together in a tapestry that records centuries of history. The Ca' d'Oro stands along the Canal, a famous palazzo which now contains a rich treasure of Venetian art. We float under the Rialto Bridge, a world-renowned city landmark. The Accademia, the largest museum in Venice, and its wooden bridge, disappear behind us as we laze past the Guggenheim Museum and pull into a berth near my hotel at the Piazza San Marco. I am in the heart of Venice.

After checking into my room, I open the windows out over the Grand Canal, sit at a desk, and study my map. The city of Venice is comprised of ten *sestieri* (areas). The interconnected districts of San Polo, Santa Croce, Castello, Cannaregio, Dorsoduro, and San Marco are comprised of numerous small islands. These areas make up the main city of Venice. The islands of Giudecca, San Giorgio Maggiore, and the Lido in the south, and San Michele to the north are all less than a three-minute ferry ride from the city center.

The lagoon is dotted with thirteen islands. The dwindling populations of each, and the complex challenges associated with their upkeep has forced the city to auction them. The winning bidder's only obligation is to completely restore the island's buildings.

The Piazza San Marco, the most famous of Venice's piazzas, is only a moment's walk outside of the hotel. Napoleon reportedly said that this square was "the most elegant drawing room in Europe." It is a splendid place. The Campanile (bell tower) reaches 320 feet into the sky above the plaza, and the Basilica of San Marco, a Byzantine treasure, faces into the square framed by a delicately carved U-shaped building. Across from the Campanile stands an intricate bell tower that now tolls the hour of 4 P.M. I am anxious to see some of the nearby islands, and I quickly board a water bus (Vaporetto, as they are called) for the island of Giudecca, within sight of San Marco.

A Walk on Guidecca

GIUDECCA IS A QUIET ISLE THAT LIES DIRECTLY SOUTH OF Piazza San Marco. It is a not-often visited place, yet it offers up a bounty difficult to find on other islands. There are quiet walkways and shady, inviting archways that lead to small, life-filled piazzas. Clothes hang from lines tied to window frames, music floats out into the still afternoon air, and neighbors knowingly greet neighbors. Several people stop an elderly woman in a wheelchair as she makes her way through a courtyard; her friends anxiously encourage her recovery.

There are a few canals that cut through the island and today, as it's an Italian religious holiday, nearly all are silent save for the lapping of water on hulls, or the pinched squabble of an occasional seagull. Much of the island is being restored. Many of the large buildings that face across the canal to San Marco are hidden behind gray fiberglass curtains and warning signs. The peace here is welcome after the cacophony of San Marco and the Vaporetto. Giudecca offers up what most Venetians find when they go home: a quiet street, clean canals, neighbors and family with whom to share time, and easy living.

There is a large, unmarked, broken down workshop on the island; no sign informs of its past purpose. There are few vestiges of any roof remaining over the inner workshops and mechanics of this ghostly place, and the skeletons of a few boats whose work was never completed line an alleyway near the building. One of the vessels is a weatherworn, sun-faded gondola. It is suspended above the stone pavements on two risers, its bow headed down the alleyway. The bright sun, showing its way through the decaying hull, interrupts the shadow it casts. It lies there, full of desire to return to the sea.

Perhaps this was a shipbuilder's place of work. If so, it's current condition offers a sobering perspective on the eroding number of craftsmen still plying their trade within Venice. Most ship and boat construction has moved to the port and harbor of Mestre on the mainland, or has disappeared altogether. This is the Venice I prefer, one without crowds, and one where you can walk quietly, discreetly, among places of peace and calm.

A man and I begin a conversation during which he says that more and more of the true born Venetians are being forced to move to the mainland, squeezed out by escalating costs for food and property. He worries that some day strangers will inhabit these special islands, especially his home of Giudecca. While such people may be in love with the city, he says, they will have shallow souls. No one, he concludes, but those born here could ever appreciate how deeply Venetians love their city in the sea.

I wander over to a canal and board a Vaporetto. As it pitches and rolls towards Piazza San Marco, I stare back at the man with whom I spoke. He wistfully leans against a pole, cigarette in hand. I wonder how long he will be able to take in such a view before the pressures of life force him elsewhere. The setting sun has powdered the evening sky a hazy violet. I disembark near San Marco.

The crowds of tourists, but not the ever-present flocks of pigeons, have fled, and I enjoy a few quiet moments beneath the Campanile. There is a constant flutter of wings, and music floats across the square from a café. What a splendid scene. Dinner and fatigue entice me back to the hotel, and I fall fast asleep to visions of the lagoon islands and the promise of another clear, warm, mid-August day.

Mosaics of Glass

MY FIRST DESTINATION THIS MORNING IS THE ISLAND OF Torcello, which lies at the far northern extreme of the Venetian lagoon. This ancient island was first settled between the fifth and sixth centuries and is home to one of the most beautiful churches in Italy. The large ferry carries me from Piazza San Marco to Torcello in about an hour, and in that hour, carries me back in time to the foundations of Venetian history.

The earliest inhabitants of Torcello were farmers. When the first church was built in the seventh century, it was the most populated of the lagoon islands. Today it is a quiet sidelight to the glories of the main city of Venice in all respects, save the mosaics in the Byzantine Basilica.

A small group of visitors and I disembark from the boat in the midst of an increasingly hot morning. Everything I see speaks of the past rather than the now. Ages ago, malaria claimed hundreds of Torcello's inhabitants. The canals filled with silt. Families abandoned farms and homes for more prosperous and healthy lives on other lagoon islands, or moved farther into the Veneto region.

There are a few signs that direct you to the Basilica. Along the pathway that leads from the boat dock to the cathedral are remnants of farms or homes that once stood on the island. Two small hotels and three cafés line one of the only remaining navigable canals. All but a few of the sixty full-time inhabitants still living on Torcello are related by blood to the generations born and raised here.

The Basilica is a splendid surprise, surrounded by large trees that provide a shady retreat from the day's heat. The cathedral, built over the foundation of the first church, was consecrated in 1008. Construction continued throughout the eleventh and twelfth centuries. The treasure inside the church is of incalculable worth, for the ceilings and walls sparkle with golden-hued mosaics. The air inside is still and damp, infused with the odor of soil. Candles flicker from candelabrum on the altar, and recorded chants fill the space.

A large column offers a hidden place from which to view the interior. The church's entire west wall is covered with the *Last Judgment*. Figures along the mosaic's base writhe amidst the fires and torments of Hell. Higher up, the figures of Christ and God are seated in judgment over those below. On the opposite wall, a weeping Madonna holds the Christ child, her figure surrounded by luminous gold tiles.

Thoughts of the incomprehensibly vast numbers of human hands and feet, of the passion and sweat that have moved through this place over the past 1,000 years, come to mind. When the mosaics were created, I wonder, did the laborers imagine that there would still be those of us who would stand to take in their work these many years later?

Did they believe that creating this work was their defining act of surrender, sacrifice, and faith? Even timeless questions with no answers must still be asked.

The walk back to the boat dock is interrupted long enough to enjoy an espresso at a café. A few visitors and locals wander by. Water laps along the sides of the canal, and a barely noticeable breeze stirs the upper reaches of the trees. It is difficult to believe that only an hour away from where I sit is the busy heart of Venice. I finish my coffee and walk back to the boat dock. From here, there is a Vaporetto that heads directly to the next island on my list, Murano.

The trip from Torcello takes us southwest across the upper expanse of the lagoon. It is approaching noon, and the breeze created by our movement along the water provides welcome relief. Murano appears as a mirage, rising above the waves of heat, shimmering above the water's surface. Deep green-leaved trees lean over ramparts above the sapphire sea; red brick and stucco walls suffuse the city with color, creating a sumptuous feast for the eyes. As soon as the boat docks I head out to discover this beautiful island.

Murano is the center of hand-blown Italian glass. Various craftsmen display their creations in windows along the main thoroughfare. I enter one of the workshops and take a seat on some bleachers set up in the rear of the building. An older, heavyset gentleman approaches a table in front of the gathered crowd and begins his labor. He opens a small furnace; a blast of heat and a flash of orange and red fill the room as he places molten glass on the end of a metal tube. He closes the furnace, brings the tube to his lips, and forces air into the bright orange globe at the other end. Within a few minutes he fashions an intricate vase, twists the colors of the rainbows around it, and places the finished piece before us on a table. The group applauds in appreciation. I approach the vase and study its stunning lines and the way it catches the light. It is amazing that so much beauty is born of fire.

I spend a few minutes exploring the display of glass for sale. A strong, focused beam of light illuminates each piece, and they glisten along dark blue velvet shelves. The light captures every hue and shade imaginable, and the reflections shower the floor with stained glass facets of color. A couple approaches the counter with their selection, a glass seashell. They smile as their purchase is completed and, once outside, they reopen the bag as if to ensure that their small treasure is really theirs. When they have returned home, I hope that they take a moment to peer into the glass and recall their moment of joy shared outside a tiny store on this beautiful island.

The isle of Torcello offers up the beauty of mosaics hidden inside an ancient church. The island of Murano offers the brilliance of light-touched glass, exposed to the sun, glistening among the shops of craftsmen who carry on a centuries-old tradition of transforming molten glass into art.

I board a Vaporetto on Murano and, as we slip south past Venice's island cemetery of San Michele, I decide to disembark at the Celestia stop. As the boat approaches the slip the city appears as quiet as Torcello. From here I will walk back through a maze of waterways and bridges to my hotel.

The small side canals are full of gondolas. These splendid handcrafted vessels have been part of Venetian commercial history since 1094. They have carried countless Doges (the political leaders of Venice), thousands of tourists, and not a small number of couples seeking the romance of the city. These boats were crafted with the kind of love, care, quality, and attention to detail that only a centuries-old tradition could provide. I wander past the church of San Francesco della Vigna, so named for the gift of a vineyard to the Franciscans who built it. I take a seat on a bench in a small park as more gondolas float by—some with passengers, others burdened with luggage or miscellaneous boxes—and think of where all these vessels are made.

Along a small byway in the Dorsoduro district across town are workshops near the church of Santi Gervasio e Protasio, in dialect know simply as *San Trovaso*. It is there that used boats are given facelifts and, on a very limited basis, new gondolas are constructed.

As I watch these brilliantly shined, coal-black boats around the city, I remember that ghostly craft, pointed into an unknown future, spending its days on a quiet side street on Giudecca. People's dreams, their idealized and hoped-for romances, come to life as gondolas gently caress the azure waves of the sea.

My journey today comes to an end at the *bacino* (basin) near San Marco. I enter the hotel and order a refreshing drink at the bar. The recommendation of the bartender will take me to a small café near the hotel for dinner. As I head up to the room, thoughts of a meal, sleep, and tomorrow fill my mind; each holds the promise of wondrous discovery.

Lido

TODAY I AM HEADED TO THE LARGEST OF THE LAGOON islands, the Lido. It is the only island that permits cars, and the only island with spectacular beaches that front the Adriatic Sea. Numerous boat slips line the main promenade near my hotel, and I eventually locate the launch that will take me over to the island.

The bow of the small craft is striped mahogany and white oak. As it lounges in its moorings, glints of sun sparkle off of the mirrored polish of varnish and wax, flashes of white-heated brilliance on an already piercingly hot morning. These boats, water taxis really, traverse the distance between Venice and the Lido every thirty minutes. As we make our way across the water, we pass glorious views of the island of San Giorgio Maggiore and the church Santa Maria della Salute. Today is a day for the sea, a day for lounging in the once-in-a-lifetime luxury of a private cabana on the sands of the Excelsior Palace Hotel.

The canals are full of other boats. Large passenger and car ferries dance around gondolas full of visitors waiting their turn to enter the small side canals that lead into the heart of the city. Other launches, freight-carrying barges and private taxis, vie for space on this vast expanse of lagoon. As we approach the Lido, the launch heads into a small passage beneath a brick footbridge. Once under the bridge, a lush paradise surrounds us.

The canal is lined with long-branched willows whose leaves glide softly across the surface of the water. Many small colorful boats are tied up along each side of the brick-lined channel, and the highest reaches along the way are rich with tropical foliage, ferns and vines, palms and hibiscus. We pass under bridges, some of which vibrate as cars pass overhead, and soon arrive at the small lagoon next to the hotel.

The building looms above me, suddenly enormous against an endless blue sky. White awnings protect private patios. Clean windows shine in the light, and a line of statues along the highest precipice surprise me with their vitality, scale, and beauty. The launch glides effortlessly alongside a covered dock.

Immaculate uniformed hotel staff greets the boat. Roses surround the inviting hallway entrance, the scent adding to the otherworldly quality of the place. Since 1907 this hotel's staff has been greeting guests with impeccable service and effortless ease. The nearby Hotel des Bains claims similar lineage, and these two grand dames of the Lido now hold sway over the social soul of the island.

The cabana assigned to me is a small room containing two chairs. White robes hang from hooks on the wall. There is a large, clean white awning, supported by two posts, that provides some shade. The canvas waves in the breeze, and the rustled murmur of other guests' voices mixes in the sultry humid air. The beach is almost empty. This is, after all, August; the majority of Italians have gone to cooler climes for vacation. A wide stretch of sand leads out into a seawall-protected bay. Various parties of swimmers and strollers walk by, collecting rocks or shells, talking, and sharing the day. On the other side of this island is the Lagoon of San Marco, the Grand Canal, and the city of Venice, where swarms of tourists vie for space, seeking impressions and memories among the city's monuments and churches. Here there are no signs or sounds of the lifeblood of Venetian commerce. There is only an occasional distant splash of waves against the shore and the snap of cloth in a gentle wind born from somewhere out in the midst of the far-distanced Adriatic.

The Lido protects the Venetian Lagoon from the Adriatic, and mariners have used the island as their first landfall, and their final view of home, before adventuring into unknown seas. Ships carried discoverers of new lands and brought the plunder of their exotic wealth back to the city. They returned past what must have been, in those days, a tropical island of small consequence. It was from these waters that the grandest armada of the time headed out to battle, Marco Polo returned with treasures from his oriental adventures, and the finest wares of the known world came to market.

Most of the visitors to the Lido, however, are more interested in the quiet laze of the sea. There is a clink of glasses in the afternoon shimmer. Waiters are moving purposefully with crisp, white, table linens, preparing for dinner guests. The snap of the cloth reminds me that the day is nearly over, that it is time to return to reality, to San Marco for dinner and rest.

The experience has been all that I could have hoped for: privacy, quiet, rest, and dreams afloat an island surrounded by the dazzling aquamarine of the sea. The launch heads out across the lagoon as the evening sky tinges with the colors of sunset. I arrive back at my room. A sumptuous dinner will mark this final evening in Venice and, later, perhaps I may stroll through the late night shadows of Piazza San Marco.

Terrace of Dreams

THE SIGNATURE RESTAURANT OF ONE OF VENICE'S GREAT hotels, the Danieli, is located on the highest floor of the building. La Terrazza (the terrace) has been serving unforgettable meals in a sumptuous setting for many years. As I am seated for dinner, the beauty of Venice sweeps before me.

It is early evening. The view encircles the expanse of the Grand Canal: south to the spires and gardens of San Girogio Maggiore; west to the translucent white façade of Santa Maria della Salute; and east to the villas of the Lido. The tables are set with white and peach-colored linens. Plates are topped with folded white napkins, each framed by a seven-piece silver service. Impeccably clean crystal glimmers. Candles flicker in Venetian hand-blown glass hurricanes, all golden flecked and wavy, which throw dancing shadows on arrangements of roses centered on each table.

I soak in this view like a warm bath: every muscle, every bone is healed by its inescapable, slow, seep; every joint loosened; every emotion freed. Light from the setting sun presses shadows across the canal off of the campanile of

San Giorgio Maggiore , and deep russet and rouge shadows pierce the water, resting there, pointing out to sea. The shadow of Santa Maria della Salute reaches nearly to the island of Giuduecca. It, too, is bathed in a sheer-silver and gold-woven wrap that will eventually turn to purple, then fade to deep, deep, azure blue. Boats and ships of every improbable description float on lime-green waters, waters that deepen from forest green to pine green, then dark emerald, and finally, ebony. Lights awaken on harbor guideposts. A circle is created in the dark lagoon, warning ships of shallow water. There is a final burst of warm evening light across the harbor as stars begin to shine down on this Venetian tapestry.

The cloudless sky above us opens up to the infinity of a diamond dusted sky. Breezes skim across the candles and tablecloths, and guests join the reverie. Night settles. Far off on the Lido a large "Campari" sign flickers on and boats that once floated in water now inexplicably float on coal black air. Only the occasional flash of light reflected on the sea's surface gives away its presence. The Venetian air softly entrances. Stars sparkle down from infinity, candles shimmer on tables of delight. Time stops. Living begins. Hearts lighten. Laughter weaves through the cooling night air.

The dinner draws quietly to a close. I know that in the days ahead, it will be reassuring to return to the memories of this place, this view, and this experience, to know that such beauty exists. Even though I will be home in a few weeks, I can always return, in some small corner of my mind, to recall this night of magic, safely held by a warm summer's eve above a city of dreams.

Late into the Venetian night, the small cafés that front the Piazza San Marco echo their music into steadily dwindling crowds. Lovers retreat to the space of their dreams and desires. The lights within the Piazza provide scant privacy to visitors who line the steps below the Campanile. The sky overhead is a blanket of deep blue; the golden spires of the Basilica of San Marco glint in the distance. Stars illuminate the canopy above as the music finds its way to a couple seated at the Café Florian.

The couple stands, walks hand in hand to the open space of the square and, to the notes that come from a group of musicians on the stage at the Café, begins to waltz. Those of us still in the Piazza gaze in wonder at the simple beauty of their dance. Their feet hardly touch the pavement. A few late night visitors gather around them to watch in splendid disbelief. Here, on pavement that has seen countless millions pass by, two lovers hold each other and move as one, smiling as they look into each other's eyes. The music's notes echo through loggias, wrap around the Campanile, and shimmer off of San Marco's domes. The couple dances within the square for a few more minutes before taking their bows to the small crowd's applause.

When I have departed the Piazza, left the tall presence of the Campanile behind, and face the fresh breeze off the Grand Canal, I imagine that the spirits of Venice's past lovers appear. They glide out over the floor of the Piazza. In the midst of their invisible dance, they remember a time when their feet touched stone under a star-studded sky. I do not turn to see them, yet I know they are there.

When I open my room's shutters and look out over the canal, I can barely hear the faint scraping of feet and the quiet murmur of conversation from phantoms I shall never meet. It is enough to know that they are there, surrendering once again to the music, the breeze, and the unimaginable beauty that is Venice.

Venetian Departure

THIS IS MY LAST MORNING IN VENICE, AT LEAST FOR THIS season. After a satisfying breakfast I walk over to the Piazza San Marco and find a shaded table from which to enjoy the view. There are a number of tour groups passing by. All are led by guides, the majority carrying umbrellas.

The enclosed walls of the Piazza create hot currents of air that move around the umbrella carriers and often catch them unaware. A few nearly lose their colorful canopies into the bright blue, limitless sky. The incessant heat raises waves of shimmering haze that hover above the pavement. Gusts of air pass through the café and bring little relief. It is becoming a scorcher of a day. The waiter brings an ice cream soda of *gelatto crema* (vanilla ice cream) and soda water. To my delight it comes with some pastries, small enticement to linger. A petite woman wearing a black dress and a veiled black hat passes by. In her left gloved hand she carries a bright white umbrella. I imagine that she is coming from, or going to, a funeral. Across the lagoon on this splendid summer day, many Venetian souls rise through the bright clouds high above the Adriatic Sea. It is a sobering thought.

As I stand in the cooling shade of a covered loggia, I know that the inescapable truths of life spin around me.

It is time to go. I reluctantly retrieve my bag from the bellmen at the hotel and board a water taxi for the train station and the trip home. As I take a seat on the Eurostar to Florence, I think back on my time here; I think about what I have learned about Venice.

What an incongruous city this is. It floats like a mirage, held above the skimming waves of the ocean, acceding to reality only when viewed close up. I can touch these stones, walks these streets, cross these bridges, and yet, when I stand apart from her, she once again becomes that mirage, that iridescent and opaque jewel that she is. How did this city appear in years past, to those from the empires of sultans and kings? They found no streets on which to ride, yet traversed canals and lagoons with unending freedom.

They rode amongst the city on gondolas that, to this day, carry cargos of commerce, romance, or hope. Late in the shroud of moonless nights, crenellated bows still pierce corners of small side waterways, slip quietly to berth along ancient pathways of water, appear as dreams in fog, or disappear entirely, hidden for days amidst the city.

Those early visitors also found a city protected by nature, further defended by her political strength and affluence. They discovered a crossroads of commerce, race, and cultures. They found the city of Venice, as she is even today, a city of limitless splendor.

The millions who visit here may never know the solitude of the island of Torcello or the quiet back alleys of Murano. Venice is, and at the same time is not, Saint Mark's Square, the Doge's Palace, and San Giorgio Maggiore. She is unique in the pattern of her isles, her waterways, her stunning and generous people, her gorgeous spires, bent and straight, that stand across islands from each other, and for her madras-rich tapestry of sea, stucco, gardens, and sky.

Before boarding my train, I pause briefly to look at the other Eurostars destined for Munich, Vienna, Nice, Monte Carlo, and Paris. My mind races ahead to their nighttime rush and morning arrivals, carrying passengers much like me who will seek slumber in beds across Europe, forever changed by this unforgettable illusion of a city. I take from her only what she somewhat reluctantly gives: an appreciation for time, for silence, for history. As the train leaves the station, I dare not turn around, for I fear that the mirage will be gone.

The train speeds on through the fertile land of the Veneto and passes through Padua and Ferrara as we head farther southeast toward Bologna and, eventually, Florence. The small alpine-like villages that so captured me on the trip to Venice come into view, south of Bologna, and I begin to plan the remainder of my time here.

The region of Tuscany offers great diversity. I look forward to exploring the historic hilltop town of San Gimignano, the seaside city of Viareggio, and the historic Monastery of Camaldoli. One of my friends from Assisi has invited me to visit her country home near a town south of Florence, and I want to visit the southern Tuscan village of Arcidosso. Settignano and Fiesole, above the valley of the Arno, offer hidden treasures as well. So, as I leave the train in Florence, I look forward to what these next few weeks hold in store.

Toscana

Baptistry

A FRIEND VISITING FROM THE STATES WANTS TO SEE THE city of Pisa and its famous Campo di Miracoli (Field of Miracles). The Campo contains the three buildings for which Pisa is best known: the Torre Pendente (Leaning Tower), the Duomo (cathedral), and the Baptistry. The town is located due west of Florence, not far from the sea. We arrive on a humid August afternoon. Crowds of visitors fill the streets, and the line to enter the Duomo appears daunting, especially in this heat. After taking some photos of the Leaning Tower we retreat to the calm, cool interior of the Baptistry.

The Baptistry has stood, nearly unscathed, for more than 750 years. The octagonal basin and statue of *St. John the Baptist* were designed and installed by Guido Bigarelli (also known as Guido da Como) in 1246. It has survived more wars than I can imagine. Its most recent brush with destruction came during World War II when Allied bombs fell on many of the buildings surrounding Campo. We are fortunate for its survival, for the Baptistry contains a gift so rare that you can't even see it: It is a place of ghostly echoes.

When I would enter this great space as a child, one of the many guards who roamed the building would stand near the baptismal font and ask for "*Silenzio!*" (silence). He would then sing out three or four very clear, separate notes of music which, when melded around the columns and reflected off the dome, would come back to my ears as full chords, as if someone had taken those individual notes and had, miraculously, wrapped them together. We heard chords and chords of music from such notes and from such voices.

My friend and I sit on one of the many steps that surround the inside circle of the Baptistry walls. As I relate the story of those childhood echoes, there is a loud "bang." A guard in an immaculate blue uniform approaches and then stands next to the font. In a booming voice he, too, commands "*Silenzio!*" I give my friend a hopeful smile, and then close my eyes. The man sings out four strong notes into the cooling dark interior and then stops. A full major chord of music reflects back to us. He does it again, in a minor key, and again the building delights our senses with magic. Once more he calls out into the dust-and-gauzed-filled light and then is done. I open my eyes and look at my friend, whose face is a mirror of delight and surprise.

We have been given a gift by this ancient place. Memories of childhood come back to me, accompanied by a sense of joy; the Baptistry still creates ghostly echoes that delight visitors as they have always done. Most importantly though, the music of the Baptistry is a connection to many things: to the shuffled feet of the believing who began coming to this place over 800 years ago; to the sculptor whose *St. John the Baptist* now stands in the center of the font; to the millions of visitors who carry memories of this place with them as they return to their homes in lands far away.

My friend arrived in August, and Florence is a city transformed. It has become a quiet, peaceful place, without hives of mopeds, horns, rush hour, or crowds. The people of Italy have gone to the sea and the mountains, and *CHIUSO PER FERIE* (CLOSED FOR VACATION) signs are everywhere. The tourist groups have changed as well. The French and Germans are more in abundance, and there is a diminishing number of Americans, mostly due to schools reopening in the States. The Florentines who remain behind seem to prefer the calm since it is easier to get around, easier to enjoy the beauty of the city, and is less stressful.

There are many other advantages to the city in August: SALE signs are everywhere, offering 10 to 60 percent off the cost of goods, be they leather, clothing, shoes, or books. Vendors in San Lorenzo's market seem much more open to bargaining. My friend and I have talked one vendor down 60 percent for a gorgeous leather carryon. The pace of commerce in all of the shops slows. Sales people lounge near registers; some fold clothing, others file nails. Lunches take a bit longer, shops reopen later than scheduled and no one seems to mind. Those who have to work during the *ferie* (vacation) find it depressing, since many friends or family members are gone. These wonderful Italians, a social culture by nature, miss those many connections, the chance to be heard by those who care. A number of shopkeepers ask us, "Why stay? Everyone else is gone!" My friend and I simply smile; she enjoys the calm, for there are fewer cars and mopeds to avoid along the narrow streets. Smaller crowds mean easier access to the city's artistic and historic treasures. What we both find oppressive is the heat.

Locals leave for the sea and the mountains because those places offer cooling breezes. The geographic position of Florence is the very reason heat piles on, magnified and held within this cauldron of a valley on the Arno. There are days and nights when little if any breeze exists and air conditioners become a near necessity. The papers this year have been full of reports of the elderly and those who suffer from asthma and other maladies succumbing alone in the incessant heat, a sad testimony to the worldwide importance of knowing your neighbors, of being close with family.

I believe that the experience of being in a less-crowded Florence outweighs any of these "costs." In spite of large groups at the Uffizi (they exist always), seeing the city settle into a less hectic, less stressful pace is wonderful. The buzz of American voices becomes overshadowed by the quiet conversations of Europeans. Cafés are more enjoyable with their peace and quiet. Over dinner on her last night, my friend and I agree that tourists should visit in August, during the *ferie*. Be prepared for heat and, in exchange, enjoy less crowded gardens, museums, and have more room to take in this timeless city.

Villages Above the Arno

MY FRIEND'S FLIGHT HOME WAS EARLY THIS MORNING. In the lonely quiet that always follows such a visit I find it therapeutic to explore. I walk over to Florence's main bus terminal and head for a nearby community.

Settignano is a small village tucked into the hills above the Arno valley. The ride takes only twenty-five minutes, yet, when I step out into the tiny piazza at the center of the town, it seems that the bustle of Florence is hours away. It is a clear, surprisingly warm August morning.

As I walk along the road from the town center, I watch the breeze catch the silver leaves of an olive grove. Waves of air pass across them like an ocean swell. A carpet of cut hay shimmers in dots of sun and shade. Farther up the hillside, dark green cypress and linden trees stand against the sapphire sky. Ancient walls and villas spot the countryside around me. A flock of doves darts in a circle above the grove and then disappears into the shadow of vegetation. The iridescent green and silver foliage moves with the air as it breathes in with one breeze, out with another. The highest branches wave a curved *Ciao*, a marvelous welcome to the gates of the Villa Gamberaia. Florentines smile when you mention the Villa, a reflection of their respect for this exquisite jewel.

A wealthy Tuscan noble, Zanobi Lapi, built the Villa Gamberaia in 1615. The majority of the main garden was well established by 1744, when Giuseppe Zocchi made the building famous in a well-known engraving. The façade of the Villa faces directly west towards Florence. Its other exposures are across the Arno valley towards Siena, into the garden itself, and through a line of cypress to a fountain. The Villa is no longer open to the public, but the garden is open nearly every day for visitors.

I ring the gate bell, a gentleman arrives to welcome me, and I enter. The approach to the Villa is along a graveled drive, through two facing rows of tall cypress trees. Once he has provided a small guide to the grounds he departs as silently as he arrived. I amble up the drive, turn right at the end of the cypresses, and stand in awe at the view. Florence spreads out before me, the domes and spires of its many churches easily recognizable in the clear morning air. It is the most beautiful view I have yet seen of the entire metropolis. I turn and begin to walk towards the garden, which, in contrast to the view out over Florence, was designed to provide a sense of expansive space within a proportionally small area.

Four water ponds are centered within a small court-yard. Lavender, roses, geraniums, wisteria, and water lilies scent the air. Along the garden's southern edge are cypresses cut and formed to resemble a loggia, their arches framing views above the Arno valley. Surrounding the pond are water irises, tall grasses, and a well-tended boxwood hedge.

There is no one else in the garden this morning and the silence is wonderful.

Sparrows flit between branches. The breeze above the valley rustles the trees and shrubs, and I can hear the sound of gently falling water. The songs of birds and the hum of bees fill the air. Who could possibly guess that we are only a few miles from the heart of Florence? I wander through the garden, enjoying the grottos, lemon trees, and roses. As I gaze over a nearby olive grove, the earth dotted with poppy blossoms, I understand why this garden holds such a place of affection in the hearts of Tuscans and Florentines. It is a place of refuge to which people escape. Visitors find peace and tranquility impossible to find in the city. The Villa Gamberaia has survived war, storms, near-total destruction during World War II, and the hands of many owners, yet retains incredible strength and beauty. I spend a last moment looking out over the distant rooftops of Florence and then wander down the cypress-lined drive. A few people wave as I return along the road back to the center of town. I board a bus in the small square. The bus travels along the spine of the hills above Settignano, and I get out in the main piazza of the village of Fiesole.

The Piazza Mino in the center of Fiesole is deserted in the midday heat of August, save for a few parked cars and a huge bronze statue. *Incontro di Teano*, (Meeting in Teano)

celebrates the 1860 meeting during which Garibaldi hailed Victor Emanuele II king of a united Italy. I walk to the walls of Fiesole's Duomo of San Romolo and begin the long, steep climb up the Via di San Francesco.

The Convent of Saint Francis, founded in 339 A.D., occupies the highest point of a hill that rises up above the town center. From the top of the stairs that lead to the Convent, I have uninterrupted views out over Fiesole, Florence, and the Arno. The small church contains only eight pews, carved in the 1500s, and several paintings from the fourteenth and fifteenth centuries decorate the interior. There is a side door from the chapel that leads to a short hallway and the sacristy. Just outside the sacristy is the entrance to a courtyard garden.

Birds call from an aviary and a single thrust of water rises from a small circular pool. Between the arches of two loggias, geraniums bloom in bright red and pink, and fallen blossoms cover the ground beneath. A few golden fish swim within the pond. It is extraordinarily peaceful. A breeze softly caresses some lavender, and bees hum on flowers.

I make my way out of the church, walk down the steep stairs to the Via di San Francesco, and eventually make my way back to the Piazza Mino in town. The bus for Florence arrives a bit later, and as it navigates the narrow and twisting roads back into the city, I reflect on how very different the experience of Italy would be without the many gardens that dot the landscape. I will be renting a car for the next several days and look forward to exploring other gardens and towns in the far corners of Tuscany.

Road to Camaldoli

ANOTHER FRIEND HAS ARRIVED FOR A FEW DAYS AND WE are determined to visit an ancient monastery northwest of Florence. Since 1046, the Camaldoli monastery has stood in the forests known as the Castelfiorentino. Saint Romualdo, the founder and leader of a group of Christian believers, sought the shelter and safe retreat of these woods. Over the years a hermitage and monastery were built to contain the ever-increasing numbers of pilgrims.

To reach Camaldoli, you must head east out of Florence along the Arno to Bagno di Ripoli, and from there, follow signs toward Poppi and Bibbiena. The heat of the day in Florence is soon forgotten as we climb up into the mountains, passing through very few small settlements along the way. The road gets increasingly steep, and the woods close in around us. On occasion we break out of the trees to breathtaking views of the Castelfiorentino. The homes we see become more chalet-like with long overhanging eaves and tiled roofs topped with stones. Artful designs, cut in the shape of hearts or flowers, decorate the shutters. It begins to look like the Alps, even though we are only forty-five minutes from the center of Florence.

Outside of Poppi, as we twist and turn our way around hills of increasing beauty, we round a curve. There are two rows of soaring cypress trees reaching up like an aisle, guiding our eyes to a rusted cemetery gate. It is so beautiful and beckoning that we stop to take in the view and enjoy an escape from the car. It is rapturously quiet. We can hear wind in the trees; birds sing as they fly above us.

The sixteen trees that line the pathway to the cemetery must have been planted over a century ago. Their gnarled and twisted branches are covered with cracked brown bark, a mirror of the hard farming land around us. The gates are held closed by a small, loosely-secured aluminum chain. We carefully unwrap it, enter, and close the gate behind us. The faces of those who rest beneath each marker stare at us from photographs placed on the memorials. All of the graves are well tended. Fresh flowers are everywhere.

The faces on the monuments speak of time. I am reminded of Masaccio, a Renaissance painter, who once wrote above a reclining skeleton: "You are now what I once was, and I am now what you are yet to be." His words, from far off Florence, seem so appropriate here. I leave the gate as I found it, making sure that I wrap the chain around the posts, and sit down on the steps. My friend strolls away, enwrapped in the quiet serenity of the scene.

There is an ornate metal cross on a pedestal centered between the trees. Two rosaries hang on it, a prayer given or a prayer answered. Once in a while a bird will sing, its melody a welcome interruption to the silence. A breeze moves the trees, and a pine cone occasionally finds its way to the ground.

There are bright yellow flowers across the road, a colorful contrast to this deep green resting place.

Down in the valley the church bells of Poppi begin to ring. The church tower is barely discernable on a far off hilltop. We are perhaps two miles from the town, and yet the bells sound near, clear, and bright. I think back to the times when the church bell measured everyone's day—the time for waking, sustenance, work, and rest. In response to the bells, a tractor comes down the road in front of the trees. The farmer driving the tractor is intent on reaching home for a meal. Perhaps he will rest a while, and then the bells of Poppi will sound again. He will rise and go to the fields. Those in the cemetery will continue their shaded hillside rest, dreaming of the days they spent among bright yellow flowers in fields of high summer.

Gardens of Collodi

EACH TIME I RETURN TO TUSCANY I MUST VISIT THE gardens surrounding the Villa Garzoni in the town of Collodi. Collodi is located about an hour west of Florence. We leave the confining streets behind and head west on the *autostrada* (superhighway). It is a gorgeous August morning as we drive into the hills of western Tuscany.

Collodi clings to the spine of a hill that rises above the Villa Garzoni. The town's main road passes by the garden entrance and eventually leads to a children's amusement center. The park was created to honor Collodi's most famous son, Carlo Lorenzini, the author of *The Adventures of Pinocchio.*

A small hut serves as the garden's ticket window. It isn't until we are past the turnstile, and some palm foliage, that the beauty unveils itself. The Villa sits high above and to the left of the garden's entrance. The scale of the space before us dwarfs even the building's massive scale. The residence was constructed in 1633 on the foundations of a medieval fortress. Design and installation took place in the mid-eighteenth century and little has changed from that original plan.

The hillside on which the garden thrives is very steep. In order to accommodate such a challenging location it was built in three distinct sections. The main level consists of two large fountains; one is now home to two bright white swans, the other is full of flowering water lilies. There is a planted Garzoni family coat of arms, and the walkways around it are flanked by terra-cotta sculptures of Roman gods. The next section is three perfectly-matched staircases that rise to a terrace. A grotto hides along the second landing. The final section has two steep stairways that lead up to a statue of *Fame* at the very top of the garden. From the tip of the shell in the figure's left hand, a large cascade of water falls nearly thirty feet into a pond at her feet. Water flows down a *scala d'aqua* (water stairway) to a catch basin near the grotto.

In size or scale, this is far from the largest garden in Tuscany. The sense of melancholy, however, is more obvious here than any other garden I have visited. Statues peek out from hedge openings above the main level of the garden, many pockmarked with signs of their age. Perhaps they have fallen prey to vandals. The oversized *Sirens* that recline on either side of the pond at the summit of the garden are moss covered; their large faces reflect the placid nature of all that they view.

On a weekday like this there are only three or four other people in the garden, and there is a feeling that this is my own private Tuscan paradise.

I descend from the heights and come to a small side gate with a green, glassless lantern. Pathways lead up to the entrance of the Villa. The shaded walkway is lined with potted hibiscus, and a few benches entice me to enjoy this cool retreat. An arched bridge over a ravine filled with bamboo of all things, is covered with rose trellises. Statues representing the seasons fill niches along the wall at the Villa's base, and when you reach the gates you feel an even stronger sense of melancholy.

The Villa, which is closed for restoration, faces the valley below Collodi. The stately two-story, stucco-covered structure displays self-confidence despite its aged façade. The chain that holds the gate closed is covered in rust, and grasses three or four feet high blanket the walkway to the main entrance. The windows are shuttered against the bright summer light. Statues peer out precariously from the roof high above. A lamp that once illuminated the gate is covered in spider webs and dust. There is an air of romantic decay about the place. You can easily see its beauty, and I look forward to the completion of the restoration.

These gardens are filled with memories of my childhood and a sense of my own history. When we lived in Italy many years ago we visited here often. I walked these same paths and took in the deep, sweet smell of life that pervades the air. I come to the top of a stair where photos were once taken of my family. The cantina at the base of the garden still has the solid wooden tables and chairs that we sat in over thirty years ago. What most encourages me about visits to this garden is that I find it always here. It is a place of stability and permanence.

I remember it on cold nights in the depths of winter; I can hear the fall of water, feel the Tuscan heat, and sense again the joys of a garden in a hillside town. In that remembering, I rediscover the feeling of peace and calm that so inhabits the grounds of the Villa Garzoni.

Gentle Hills

AN ENGLISH ACQUAINTANCE IN ASSISI HAS INVITED me to visit her country home about an hour south of Florence. She is, among other things, a wonderful water-colorist. She has lived in Italy for over forty years—in Rome actually—seeing to people's needs through the Food Agricultural Organization of the United Nations. She found her country house through friends of friends of friends in the early 1970s. At the time it was purchased, land and all, the house was in sad condition, run down by years of neglect and lack of love. She has transformed it.

Her home sits off of the main thoroughfare of a nearby town at the end of a winding, often steep, dusty road. Along the way, I pass a working farm. Farther on is a villa that once belonged to a landlord before his holdings were broken into leaseholds. The villa seems a beautiful, quiet retreat. Just past it I turn left. If I were to miss that turn I would end up at what she calls the "wrong house," so named because so many people have inadvertently discovered it. I soon come upon the sign for her country home.

The house sits next to two huge cypress trees. There is a loggia for a garage. Small steps lead to a tiny porch with a table and two chairs. She greets me as I drive up, both arms waving over her head, and then gives me a big hug and double-cheek kiss in welcome.

"Well," she smiles, "at long last you've arrived. I've kept hoping that 'the boy' would come and, indeed, he has."

Her eyes are bright and she wears a pair of neon-and-rainbow-striped glasses that fade to white at the base of each lens. They lighten her face like the sun, complimenting the deep blue of her eyes. After niceties we settle on the terrace off the dining room.

"Years ago," she tells me, "I had this porch built out as you see it today. It used to be all closed in, one big room, and seemed to beg for light. We worked on it over a summer and *voilà*." Her simple description doesn't do justice to the stunning beauty of the terrace and the view. Two busts, one of a friend she did years ago and one given to her by an artist who didn't want it anymore, stand at the left and right corners of the loggia. The three main arches frame a view across her vineyards, up into the hills of Chianti, and beyond to villages and villas of searing beauty.

We pass the afternoon chatting about how she found the house, how long it has taken to fix up, the creation of wine, of olive oil, and of her years of travel to and from this splendid retreat. Eventually, she retires to her room for a nap and I take my camera to stroll the land.

Succulent magenta-red grapes shine in the sun, offset by white-green grapes of translucent wonder. Each one is different, each one sparkling in the heat of the August Chianti sun. Olives burden the tree branches more heavily now, and soon enough the late fall harvesters will arrive, all with netting and hydraulic "shakers," strong backs, and tender care. I take picture after picture of nature's unending show of shadow and sun, of green, umber, mauve-purple, and soft light. I stop to think of the families, years from now, who will be blessed to pour out this sun and color into a glass. Will those lucky few, probably miles and many memories from here, taste the months of absorbing light, care, and the shade of an Italian hillside?

Late in the afternoon, we sup on bright red chunks of garden fresh tomatoes and basil, and white cuts of mozzarella and Asiago cheese covered in a light broth of olive oil and balsamic vinegar. She nonchalantly tosses the pits of black olives over her shoulder. They disappear over the precipice of the loggia into the yard below. Perhaps she hopes that nature will provide her more olive trees for shade and fruit.

It must be difficult for her to be here alone, at the end of a long dusty road, deep in Chianti. She is, however, a resilient lady. Over forty years ago she packed up and moved from England to Rome, found work, and created a good life for herself and her friends. She'll get by just fine.

We watch shadows lengthen in the hills above and around us and, as evening gives way to night, we both express deep affection for the beauty of Tuscany. With the new moon rising in the east, I bid her a good-bye and express hope that there shall be more chances to meet, to laugh, to spend time in the sun amidst her gentle hills.

As I drive north up the *autostrada* towards Florence, I wonder if another day will ever come when I can return to experience her hospitality and generous good heart. I trust so, and, as I park the car and walk back to my apartment, I say a quiet thanks for such people and for such a place.

There remain three places in Tuscany I must visit: San Gimignano, a splendid hill town to the south; Arcidosso, a medieval treasure at the far southern extreme of the Tuscan region, and San Galgano, the ruins of a once magnificent cathedral. Weather permitting, tomorrow I will head to Arcidosso.

Places of Hope

MY DREAM OF OWNING PROPERTY IN TUSCANY REMAINS, at best, a distant one. However, a recent listing for a farmhouse piques my curiosity and I call for details.

"Yes, it is still available," says the agreeable owner. "I will meet you at the garden near the Arcidosso city gate tomorrow at noon. I can have you follow me up to the property." I readily agree and call on an Italian friend who is more than pleased to offer his time for the trip.

The town is an easy hour and thirty minutes south of Florence. There is little traffic on this beautiful Sunday morning as we drive through the hills of Tuscany. The routes between Rome and Florence are dotted with numerous small villages. Along the main road we see many tiny hill towns above us. My friend says that many of these places suffered a great deal during the wars and political unrest that so typified life during the Middle Ages and Renaissance.

The approach to Arcidosso is along a winding road that twists above the Orcia River, and we can make out the lofty battlements of the town as we approach. Close up, the city walls still show the damage of those ancient conflicts. You can easily see scars from cannon balls and black soot from fires. A few crenellated towers push their aged shoulders high on either side of the main gate.

We park next to a garden of lavender and wildflowers that bloom near the ancient gates of the city. The owner, Christina, arrives. After exchanging greetings, we sit for a few moments to get acquainted and enjoy the view out over the valley.

Christina relates some of the area's history.

"This is a very spiritual place," she says. "A strong willed Christian leader of the twentieth century, Davide Lazzaretti, founded a colony of believers up near the rocky summit of the mountain behind the town." She points to our right across the valley. There is a large white building easily visible on the slopes of Monte Labbro, the highest peak in Southern Tuscany. "It is *Merigar*," she says. "It means 'Fire-Mountain,' and is the largest Buddhist monastery in Italy. The Dalai Llama has been there to visit."

As we stare across the verdant valley, a nearby flash of light catches my eye. We are suddenly surrounded by hundreds of butterflies. The direct midday sun reflects off of their wings, and we watch as they land on blooms of lavender, quietly moving about their business.

"This place has always been a holy place," she continues. "That is partly what brought me here many years ago. I believe that there are wonderful and positive spirits here. That belief has carried me through many difficult days. I am selling this house because I must move on now. Life changes." She shrugs her shoulders.

I can't help but notice the longing in her eyes as she stares at the opening and closing wings around us.

"The spirits that guide us are here always. Even in these gardens of Arcidosso." She rises and goes towards her car. "Shall we go up to the house?"

We follow as she drives the twisted, graveled road up to her home. She kindly gives a tour of the house and studio. It is an amazing place, lovingly restored over the years of her life. The view out over the valley is astonishing, breathtaking. We can see for miles, down into the valley below Arcidosso, and as far away as the forest-covered slopes of distant mountains. After coffee and further chat, we thank her for her hospitality and, very reluctantly, depart. We wish her well.

Upon returning to Florence, the complexity of owning such a home overpowers my dream—at least for now. Christina tells me that she understands and invites my continued contact with her via email. Some months after returning home, I receive correspondence from her. She writes that she sold the house and moved to a smaller town a bit north of Arcidosso. In the last sentence of the letter she tells me that in all of the times that she's been back to Arcidosso, she has never again seen the number or variety of butterflies that we saw that summer day. She writes, "Perhaps the spirits were encouraging you to your dream, to live here. Someday I believe it will come true." I hold fast to that hope.

"Do you know of the cathedral ruins of San Galgano?" my friend asks as he drives us back down the main road to Florence. I tell him that I have only read of it. He smiles and says, "Well, then, we must go. They are too beautiful to miss."

We rise into the hills south of Siena. He turns the car onto a small road in the tiny town of Macereto, and we head west. In the hill town of Monticiano are signs that direct us to San Galgano.

The approach to this marvelous medieval ruin is across a large heat-beaten field. A row of cypress trees frames the long dusty walk towards what was the main entrance to the cathedral. There is a sense of melancholy, a shoulder-slumping weariness that seeps into you as you approach the walls. The empty shell of the church is all skeletons and no flesh.

In 1148, a young knight named Galgano was inspired to turn away from violence and knighthood. In an act of surrender to his faith, he attempted to break his sword against a stone. Instead, it slipped into the heart of the rock. He took it as a sign from God and began his spiritual journey as a hermit. Over time his followers built a hermitage. The Chapel of Montesiepi, an oratory, was also built above the sword and stone. In 1185, four years after Galgano's death, he was elevated to sainthood.

The ruins of what once was the Cathedral of San Galgano stand empty in the valley below the Chapel.

The church, started in the year 1218 and finished five years later, was greatly influenced in style by the Cistercian monks who came from France to support the mission of

Galgano. The small settlement around the church became a place of pilgrimage for earnest Christians throughout the thirteenth and fourteenth centuries. Access to the settlement, just off the main road connecting Siena and Grosseto, made it an easy target for plunder. In 1397, a mercenary army from England sacked all of the buildings and took the majority of the church's treasures.

The Cistercian's favorable affiliation with the Sienese made it an easy target for the armies of Florence, and conflicts between the city-states of Siena and Florence added to the Cathedral's demise. Safe routes to and from the Cathedral were eventually cut off. The church suffered through a steadily decreasing population of monks. By 1550, only five monks remained to care for the Cathedral and hermitage and, by 1786, when the seventy-five-foot bell tower collapsed into the nave, only one monk remained.

The roof is now long gone, as are the stained-glass windows that once illuminated the interior. The brick frames of what were large round windows are now empty, the perfect place for a sparrow or swallow to pass some time. Most of the stone flooring of the building was removed once the Cathedral no longer served as a place of worship. What remains is a shell of holy labor, surrounded by glorious forests of oak. Dust swirls around the battered columns. The main altar, now a simple stone slab, provides some scale to what the church must have been at the height of its glory. As you walk the grounds, there are vistas where only the upper reaches of the Cathedral can be seen, and I imagine the days when the church was surrounded by pilgrims.

"What do you think?" my friend asks. I can only shake my head. The word "magnificent" seems unworthy to describe this glorious ruin. We are silent as the car rumbles down the gravel drive and heads back towards Florence. I reflect on our visit.

The passing of such a place is full of poetic sadness. The sweat and care of the laborers who created it has long since melded into stone. Windows were carted away and melted down for other uses. The wooden pews and the artwork that once graced the interior were dispersed across Europe or destroyed. The Cathedral of San Galgano once rivaled England's Salisbury Cathedral, or France's Rheims Cathedral. Today it stands empty. What fills that space is faith, and as we renter the gates of Florence a memory settles into me that I shall never forget. It was the voice I heard, whispered by a simple hermit, saying "I believe."

Notes from a Well

WHEN I AWAKEN THE NEXT MORNING THE SUN IS CLEAR and bright in a cloudless blue sky. This is the perfect day to visit San Gimignano. As I drive through the nearly empty streets of Florence and head southeast towards Siena on the winding *autostrada*, I think of the many times I have visited this superb medieval hill town. As popular as it is, I never notice the crowds, never wish for more quiet than it can provide. It is enough to spend time in its ancient byways and enjoy the views from a fort high above the city. I round a bend in the road and, quite suddenly, she appears.

The hills of central Tuscany thrust San Gimignano up, shouldering it high above the valleys that surround it. Towers spike the sapphire sky and the sun sparkles against the city walls; it is an apparition of extraordinary beauty. I park my car near the ramparts of the town and make my way through the Porta Romana, the oldest of the city's few gates. As I stroll up the Via San Giovanni, I pay little heed to the many wonderful shops that line the steep, cobbled road. I seek the quieter side streets of this wondrous town. As I approach the main piazza, harp music tempts me to enter a small archway.

When I enter I cannot find the source of the music. I only know that behind the shelter of a well house someone is creating notes of pure rhapsodic beauty. The music moves around the open space. A small, mesmerized group of fortunate listeners stands nearby. I stand, awestruck, transported to some other century when such music was the fare of courts and kings, barons and bishops. I finally move, ever so slowly, around the well house.

A man sits facing away from the center of the square so that the music from his harp is reflected off the walls. The golden instrument rests on his shoulder. A flock of swallows and sparrows rest on a high row of terra-cotta roof tiles, nearly motionless. They seem to be held in the thrall of these notes and the simple warmth of the sun. I leave through the archway and continue to walk up the steep street that leads to a fortress, ages old, above the town center.

The views from this highest point of the city offer unobstructed vistas in every direction over numerous valleys and distant hills. A few towers, which once numbered in the hundreds, have survived the centuries of conflict that this town has known. They stretch up into the sky, encircled by swallows, marked by a few plants, heated by the sun. They remind me of fingers, somehow, that scratch at the Tuscan sky. As I stare through brilliant, clean air, the songs of the harp from below the parapets fade away. I hope for some other music to accompany the view. A few minutes later, a gentleman arrives and sets up a harpsichord near an olive grove. His music fills the void as a slight breeze rustles the vines and trees in the center courtyard. A nearby gate entices me with more splendid views and I am drawn out and away from the music. Slowly, slowly, I walk down to the car and head back to Florence.

I drive onto the shoulder of the road that twists through the valley and stand for a few moments to take it in one last time. I cannot recall when I first surrendered my heart to San Gimignano, this glory of towers that thrusts up and touches the endless azure sky. I only know that its beauty and mystery always enrich my experiences in this marvelous country.

Return to the Sea

THE RIVER ARNO REACHES FOR THE SEA FROM ITS origins high in the mountains east of Florence. It longs for boundless freedom as it tumbles past the towns of the Tuscan frontier and cuts through the heart of the city. Its pace slows as it flows on to Pisa, eventually melding its silt and history-laden waters with the azure depths of the Mediterranean. Not far north of the city of Pisa, along the coast, is the town of Viareggio. I have accepted an invitation to visit friends who live in a small village in the hills above the city.

It is only a ten-dollar, one-hour train ride from the Santa Maria Novella station in Florence to the coast. There are a number of *Treni Regionali* (regional trains) that leave from tracks less crowded than the Eurostar's—those luxurious, swift, silver marvels that crisscross Italy and the entire continent of Europe. The regional trains are simpler. They are designed for the singular task of transport between the larger cities of Italy and the small towns that surround them.

At 9:40 A.M., I board my train and take a seat in a nearly empty car. My impressions of the outskirts of Florence are not unlike suburbia everywhere: tall faceless flats of building after building; clothes hung out to dry; many porches occupied by washing machines. Some porches boast small container gardens. Outside of Florence's center we stop at Sesto Fiorentino and then head out into the open plains to the west. Soon we travel through golden fields of sunflowers. Deep green grapevines flash by. Farmhouses blink past as the train picks up speed. Some small town stations stand nearly empty along the tracks as the train continues its western journey.

The next stop is Prato, a city that has, since the thirteenth century, created fabrics and textiles for the world. There are records in Prato, dating from the 1400s, when the Medici family ordered cloth from its mills. Trains bound for Milan, Bologna, and Genoa enter and leave the station as we await our departure for Pistoia, the next stop. We head a bit north, and enter the foothills of the Apennines. We rush along canals. A landscape business fills the windows of the train for many minutes; oak, olive, linden, pine, and cypress trees, and every other bush, shrub, and plant you can imagine stand row on row as we pass. The train continues to climb above a plain of verdant green, and we soon arrive in Pistoia. This station is like so many others across Italy, formed of bronze and marble. Cafés front the arrival and departure area. There is a room for luggage, a main lobby, and the ever-present track numbers (*Binario 1, Binario 2*).

As we near the next stop, Montecatini Terme, the abruptness of the hills is more pronounced. High above the train are many villas, castles, vineyards, and olive groves. Since the days of Roman antiquity, Montecatini Terme has attracted the ill and the infirm, offering sulfurous heated waters to cure and renew. The financial resources of this town are obvious in the train station. There is gorgeous light-tan marble, custom brass railings, intricate cut-glass doors, and plants everywhere. It's truly a stunner.

The train heads west again and very quickly arrives in Lucca, home to one of the oldest cathedrals in Tuscany. We are only in the station for a few minutes. Shortly after we leave, the train enters a long tunnel, and when it bursts out of the other side we are within sight of the sea. The air is sweeter and fresher, and as we approach Viareggio, the sun appears from behind the clouds. Rays of light glint off of villas and villages high in the far off mountains. Fabio Baudone, whose family has run a famous restaurant in Florence (Ristorante Bibe) for many generations, greets me at the station and tells me we are going up to his friend's house before coming back down to the sea. I find myself standing in front of a large silver motorcycle, my friend holding a spare helmet. We are off. Memories of my child-hood in Tuscany wash over me.

It was 1958. Our family and friends crowded a small balcony at a downtown hotel in Viareggio to watch a *carnevale* parade, a pre-Lenten celebration, move through the streets that front the coast. I vividly remember looking eye to eye with floats (all flowers and gears and eyes with eyelashes out to forever), watching the crowds on the street enjoying the parade. The weather wasn't cold, that day, as I recall.

Today, it's hot, and even though I do not recognize the piazza in front of the station, I carry my memories with me on this new adventure. Viareggio is full of tropical plants: palms, hibiscus, and other flowers of indescribable colors poke up and out from every planting and every balcony. As we turn out of the city, the countryside opens up and we are headed along a canal where workers are bent in their labor. We round a traffic circle, turn to the right, and suddenly begin to climb.

The road becomes a sinuous curve where Fabio slows, brakes, and turns, accelerates, slows, brakes, turns, and accelerates. The air freshens as we climb, and between villas that line the road there are increasingly spectacular views. We move up and into the hills high above the flat plain fronting the sea. The smell of burnt umber, of linden trees and flowering vines fills the air. In the little village of Bargécchia we stop behind a large truck and wait while a delivery of bottled water is made at the local store. We finally arrive in Mómmio Castello, a very small village perched on the spine of a hill high above Viareggio.

The house I am visiting is hidden off of a small street in the town. I am introduced to the owner, Joachim Temme, and he offers to take me on a tour. There is one small portion of the house that he is restoring for an apartment; you can't imagine. The walls appear to be standing by the good graces of God and there are old, very old, timbers fallen in. It is full of rusted pots. "This is how the whole house looked when it was purchased. I found two brothers from the town who took one year to restore the main house."

The finished product is awe-inspiring. The house consists of four levels: a garden below the house; a level containing the kitchen and a den, and two levels of living room and bedrooms. The garden tumbles down the hillside below the house. Hydrangeas of every conceivable hue dot the grounds; roses climb into clear blue skies. Geraniums line walkways and stairs. There is a water garden, an herb garden, two large olive trees, and a loggia covered in bright neon-purple bougainvillea. Emerald-green ivy climbs the walls. He has installed two small sculptures. One is a woman who, knees pulled against her chest, stares out across the view, the other a bronze torso that stands atop a column on the dining terrace. Another friend, Norbert Weinheimer, joins us at the conclusion of the house tour. We pack up the car and head to the sea.

Most of the cleanest beaches in Italy are private. In order to use them you either join for the season or pay each time you visit. The public beach, near a nature preserve, is much less crowded. Most people opt for the free beach. It is a long walk out to the water on a recently built, raised wooden walkway. As we stroll out towards the sea, I think back those many years to a time when, as a child, I had no inkling of the life before me, nor of the day I would return. We find a quiet section of beach, put up umbrellas, and stretch out on the sand. My eyes are drawn out along the shore, to the thousands of shells that have washed up, and I lazily select a few for family back home.

The day lingers long in the hot sun. We talk, laugh, and eventually doze off. I take a quick swim in water surprisingly warm and clean, return to the welcome shade of the umbrellas, and stretch out.

I think of the civilizations that have been carried by these waters. The Greeks, Romans, Egyptians, and many others, have navigated this ocean, their fleets burdened with cargo or plunder. The Mediterranean is known, among mariners, as home to some of the most treacherous storms in the world. The lives of many sailors have been claimed by the unpredictable nature of this sea. There are no clouds above us on this splendid afternoon, and the ocean before us is calm.

Vendors ply the beach with cold drinks, fresh food, jewelry, and towels. We talk to a few, bargain some good deals, and then lay back to bask in the sun. As I begin to doze, I am filled with appreciation for the gift of this day along the sea. A child and his mother stroll by along the shore. Many years ago, this country was my home. My Italian season will soon come to a close and I anticipate visits to the nearby city of Pisa and other places of memory before heading back to the States. For now it is more than enough to find slumber with visions of the azure blue Tyrrhenian Sea accompanying me in sleep.

Last Train to Pisa

TRAINS ARE THE LIFEBLOOD OF ITALIAN LIFE. THE MAZE of tracks that crisscross the land trace connections of culture, history, and family. I have traveled on the trains between Florence and Pisa from the time I was a child. I am headed back to Pisa one last time to solve a mystery.

From Florence's Santa Maria Novella Station the train heads to the Florence-Rifredi Station. It used to be that you could only get to the Italian Express trains, the *Rapido*'s, here at Rifredi. Now the Eurostars come in and out from the main station, and Rifredi has become a somewhat sleepier local stop. As the train gains speed, it passes the outskirts of Florence, moves steadily faster past garden plots and high-rise apartment buildings, and passes under the suspension bridge linking the suburb of Scandicci with the airport.

The train traces the northern side of the Arno, and it sways on the track like the pendulum of a clock. Its click-clack staccato takes me back to the Tuscany of my childhood, spent in the small seaside village of Terrannia. We glide into and out of the villages of my youth: Pontaderra, Montelupo, Empoli. Signa, across the river from Lastra, was once a small village, but is now a large bedroom community for workers in Florence and nearby Montelupo. We travel on to the huge river bend deep below Artimino (home of the Medici Villa Reale La Ferdinanda, also known as "The Villa of a Hundred Chimneys"), through Compignano—no stop—and course along the reed-lined riverbanks. Olive groves scramble up hillsides, villas perch above them, and always there is the presence of the Arno that, like those of us on this train, seeks Pisa. We cross the Arno outside of the station in Montelupo and begin to travel along the southern side of the river.

Montelupo. It was here that our family would explore shops brim-full of ceramic wonder: donkey cart planters; pitchers; plates that were, and still are, the colors of the Tuscan countryside. We would often eat in a small restaurant, perched above the river, where the corner fireplace was full of grouse turning on a spit. A huge liquid-green jar full of olives, and a cold case full of cut meats, cheeses, and vegetables occupied the center of the room. That restaurant is still there, the cold case is still full of delights, and the fireplace is cold now; it is, after all, summer.

We move out of Montelupo and head along the river to Empoli, the center of commercial Italian glass manufacturing. Here, those many years ago, we purchased a set of dark emerald-green glasses, some large for water, some smaller for wine. They are the best, heaviest, most substantial glassware we ever bought. My family still uses them to this day.

The train stops in Empoli, and the smells of the rail yard unexpectedly awaken more memories: the odor of hot brakes; the smell of heat as it rises from the asphalt of the platform; an occasional waft of dark, rich coffee from the trackside café; and the ever-present smell of cigarettes. The train pulls out of Empoli and we head directly for Pisa Centrale. Pisa is where, years upon years ago, we nearly missed a connection between trains jam-packed with Italian skiers. It is the city where our beloved landlord, a doctor, still lives in the family palazzo on Via Medicio direct on the Arno in the heart of town. I notice children playing soccer in a newly-planted field just outside of Empoli, and they remind me that my journey, the one that I thought was coming to an end, is just beginning.

The land outside of Empoli opens wide, the mountains to the north invite and recede into the distance. They hold the promise of towns like Carrara, Viareggio, the Cinque Terra, and beyond, the French Riviera and Alps. The train continues to trace along the southern side of the River Arno for a few more minutes, and then we arrive into Pisa Centrale Station.

The journeys of life have a beginning. This journey started near Pisa, as a youth of first and second grade where Italian was a mandatory course, and the language of these beloved people filled my ears and enriched my life. This is a journey where I leave a train, where a mystery is solved. This day holds, as has the entire summer, great promise and wonderful adventure. I walk out of the station into the glaring August light of the Piazza Vittorio Emmanuele II. I carry with me a black-and-white photograph of a shop, and the hope of finding "G. Barsanti and Sons."

The walk from the train station to the Duomo and Leaning Tower of Pisa takes you through what is now a pedestrian-only corridor of shops, restaurants, and covered arcades. It is a cooling walk in the heat of this August day. I pass several discount music shops, restaurants, and clothing stores. There are also a few cafes and the ever-present Tabaccheria where you can buy cigarettes and city bus tokens. The approach to the river at the Lungarno Galilei, a street that celebrates a famous son of this city, greets me with a breeze and spectacular views up and down the river. In Florence, the river moves with great purpose, crossing two splash-ways with fervor. Here in Pisa the river is more subdued, quieter and wider as it seeks the open waters of the sea. It seems reticent to release itself from this rich land of history and beauty.

Once across the bridge, my walk takes me to the Piazza della Cavalieri, the place of horsemen. There is a large building on the north side of the Piazza covered in *sgraffito*, a decoration scratched into wet plaster. The structure was built to house the Cavalieri di San Stefano, an order of knights created by a Medici ruler at a time when the city was under Florentine rule. It is now part of the University of Pisa. The Piazza is quiet. A few strollers take their time in the shadows, and a man on a bicycle peddles past. As I near the Campo dei Miracoli (Field of Miracles), the Leaning Tower and the dome of the Duomo come into view.

This day, however, is not for those sights. I find the black-and-white photograph, taken in 1957, of a shop fronting the Campo. The name of the shop owners, "G Barsanti e Figli" is clearly legible in that photo, and I have come with hopes of finding the store. At the corner of the Via Roma and the Piazza del Duomo, I find what I believe to be the same shop.

I enter. There is an older gentleman at the counter.

"Excuse me, I am looking for Signor Barsanti, please."

He looks around and points to a man with glasses, slightly graying hair, a small moustache, a slight build, and an open, friendly face. I approach him.

"Signor Barsanti?" I inquire.

"Yes," he says, tentatively, almost expecting some sort of problem.

"My name is Mark," I start, shaking his hand. "I apologize for disturbing you. I have come to give you something. From 1956 to 1959 our family lived in Terrannia when my father was working in Livorno."

"Yes?" He smiles, still a bit confused.

I show him the photograph. "This picture was taken during that time. Is this, indeed, the same store?"

His face brightens and he smiles, widely. "My goodness! No, this is not that store. The store in this photograph was closed in 1971." Then he gets very animated.

"I remember this! I remember this store as it appears here, as a boy. I worked here as a boy! What a wonderful picture!"

I smile back. "Well, my mystery is solved and I want to give you this picture as a gift, a remembrance, for both of us."

He smiles, holds out his hand, and says, "Many, many thanks. This is so very kind."

I pause, and then ask him, "Do you, by any chance, know the Barale family? They are from Pisa and he was our—how do you say in Italian—landlord when we lived here." The look on his face becomes part shock, part joy, and part surprise.

"Well, yes" he says. "How very strange. Yes, Dr. Barale delivered my second granddaughter here, in Pisa."

Now it's my turn for shock and surprise.

"Dr. Ettore Barale?" I ask.

"Yes," he says, "exactly."

When we lived in Terrannia those many years ago the elder Dr. Barale was our landlord. Ettore, his eldest son, is now a successful doctor practicing in Pisa and at a nearby military base, Camp Darby.

As I smile a good-bye to him, I say "Please say hello to Dr. Barale when you next see him. I have hopes of seeing him before I leave Italy next week."

"I will, certainly," he replies.

Prior to departing the store, I glance back at Mr. Barsanti. He is standing next to one of the display cases in his store, staring into the memories that the photograph awakened in him.

One of the many museums surrounding the Campo di Miracoli is the Museum of the Sinope. The term *sinope* refers to the outlines, or "cartoons," placed upon plaster walls prior to being painted in color. In that museum there is a large work of the circles of heaven. Its outline is faintly visible and you must stand for minutes to take in what it must have looked like in its full and splendid color. The piece reminds me of the circles in our lives, of how people, cultures, and generations can intersect each other in the most extraordinary and surprising ways. A photograph taken in 1957 brings together two cultures, intersects many lives, and connects us to the greater family of humanity.

As I board the train to return to Florence it occurs to me that life can be like a train, often is. We hop aboard, and someone takes us where we think we are supposed to go. The train lulls us; the fresh air mesmerizes us. We breathe deep and are wrapped in a hypnotic trance, into the sway of our heartbeats, the motion of the days. The train moves in and out of stations: youth, graduation, marriages, divorces, relationships, and health problems. If we do not awaken, if we do not learn to get off the train—to change trains—we may find ourselves at the end of some long, lonely set of tracks. We may be sitting in an empty train car, surrounded by a field of bowed-over sunflowers awaiting the harvest (a harvest of regret) wondering what happened to the trip and where we are. This last train to Pisa carries me back to Florence, a mystery solved. I hope that in the days and years ahead I remember to change trains, remember that the trip can pass too quickly, and remember that what matters most is the common bond in all of us to family, love, and life.

Epilogo

THE LAST DAY OF AUGUST, AND STREETS ARE ONCE AGAIN crowded with cars, hives of mopeds, and Vespas. The sleeping jewel awakens, the *ferie* (the annual vacation) ends. The number of American tourists has continued to dwindle, and German, French, Dutch, and Japanese tourists are more in abundance; in total, though, there does not seem to be quite as many tourists as earlier in the summer. The line at the Uffizi is much shorter than earlier in season, the line for the Accademia not much past the corner on the Via Degli Alfani.

The city awakens from its late summer slumber and abruptly opens its eyes through a haze of disorienting noise and crowds. It is lumbering back to life, much to the disappointment of a few of us who have weathered the heat and deep humid days of absence.

The mood of the city is changing; people who have bronzed their bodies on beaches along the Mediterranean coasts, those who have breathed fresh mountain air in Alps and Apennines, now breathe city air, now reluctantly fade into offices. They move back into the moods of workers everywhere, who subjugate their yearnings for freedom, and for now must live their lives for the omnipresent "them." My season in Italy is coming to a close. Schools start up again on September 10, and we, the *quasi-Fiorentino*, will also move ourselves back into days and worlds of the almighty "them."

Saturday. September. The winds have changed and we enjoy our first glorious day for weeks. It is clear enough to count the crenellations on the church tower in Fiesole, and the hills north of the city are a splendid green and tan with terraced grapes and red village rooftops. It is such a welcome relief from the still, hot air of only a few days ago. There is a faint scent in the wind. It carries something from the east, a sense of change. Leaves brushed against my feet as I strolled through a piazza near my apartment this morning, small curls of autumn color that projected my thoughts ahead to cooler days. Those days will come to fruition well after I leave.

Today, I simply enjoy the welcome change. I sit in a small park on my street, breathe this fresh purified air, and cool myself in the shade of trees, knowing that unrelenting change comes soon to the heart of Tuscany.

The rains have arrived, as if on schedule, this first week of September. Gusts of wind billow curtains and bang window shutters. The rain pelts umbrellas and flattens flowers. Cypress trees blow restless and other trees begin dropping their leaves.

Earlier today, I walked along a narrow, ancient street with high-shouldered walls bordering each side, presumably built to protect some unseen beauty within. Around a corner leaves fell, shimmering gold in the mid-afternoon light. How strange it seems for autumn to announce herself so abruptly in Florence, where the season has passed by too suddenly, too softly, too swiftly.

Many people have walked the streets of the city these past months, their footfalls echo still at the Uffizi, Academia, and Bargello. Hands which once touched stone and art return to more common labor in Tokyo, Paris, Denver, or Sydney. Memories were created by friend's visits, and stories of past Italian adventures will be shared over winter fires and spring walks. However, the rains of autumn have arrived.

What can never be washed from the walls, the streets, the bridges, and towers of this beloved city are the memories that visitors have carried away with them. Come winter, spring, or another far-distant summer, these can never be replaced, nor should be.

Once again, life is reduced to a few small shipping cartons filled with the plunder of a season. My boxes will soon find their way across the Atlantic, headed for the United States and home. I never, ever, really leave Florence, Tuscany, or Italy. Like so many others who have found a home for their souls here, I leave bits and pieces of mine behind. Regardless of where I am, I am always connected to these hills, these people, and this culture.

All I need do is close my eyes: the shaded beauty of the Boboli Gardens; the scented paradise of a friend's garden above Viareggio; the sun-dotted tables of a café in Assisi; or the quiet majesty of ancient mosaics high up in an island church near Venice fill my heart. Couples waltz through a Venetian piazza, friends greet me in a neighborhood café, small sparrows sit on the benches of the Piazza Repubblica, and swallows ballet in the onrush of sunset above the Arno. The music of timelessness floats out of the Uffizi Loggia, rises above the towers of Santa Croce, and finds its way to lovers on the Ponte Vecchio. Words spoken in affection deepen bonds; they tighten our human experience and connection, enrich our souls, find favor in our memories, and provide a place of retreat.

As surely as my plane lifts over the Arno valley on the journey home, this country will continue to invite me in. She will seduce with her beauty and her never ending hold on the history of a changing world, a world that will always find itself smiling at the mention of one simple word: *Italia.*